# TIGER-WALLAHS

# TIGER-WALLAHS

ENCOUNTERS WITH THE MEN
WHO TRIED TO SAVE THE
GREATEST OF THE GREAT CATS

BY GEOFFREY C. WARD
WITH DIANE RAINES WARD

*Preceding pages*: A tigress begins her evening hunt beneath the ramparts of the fort at Ranthambhore National Park in Rajasthan.

FIRST EDITION

*Designed by Wendy Byrne*

**Library of Congress Cataloging-in-Publication Data**
Ward, Geoffrey C.
   Tiger Wallahs : encounters with the men who tried to save the greatest of the great cats / by Geoffrey C. Ward with Diane Raines Ward. — 1st ed.
       p.    cm.
   Includes bibliographical references.
   ISBN 0-06-016795-5
   1. Tigers—India.   2. Wildlife conservationists—India—Biography.   3. Wildlife conservation—India.   4. Endangered species—India.
   I. Ward, Diane Raines.   II. Title.
QL737.C23W37    1993
599.74′428—dc20                          92-56245

93 94 95 96 97 ❖/RRD 10 9 8 7 6 5 4 3 2 1

FOR BILLY

AND FOR FATEH

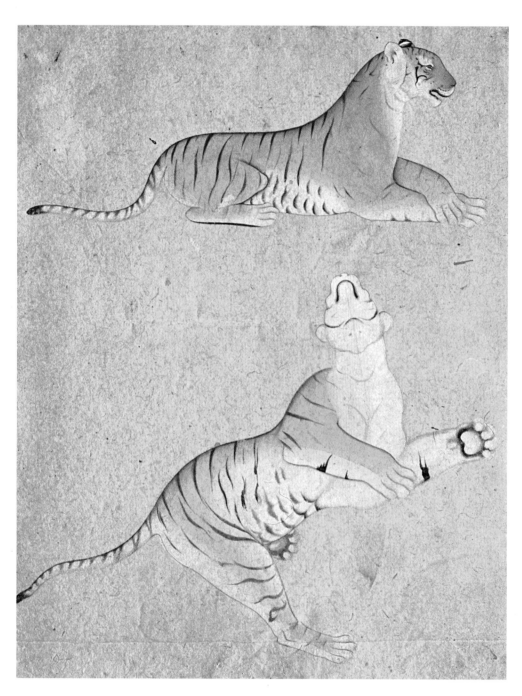

Studies of a captive tiger, painted by an unknown eighteenth-century artist to
delight the tiger's owner, the ruler of one of the princely states in the Punjab hills.

# CONTENTS

A British hunter finds himself uncomfortably close to his quarry
in an ivory miniature from Patiala State, circa 1892.

When I set out to write this book almost ten years ago, I had something quite different in mind—a set of profiles of several of the Tiger-Wallahs, or tiger-men, who devoted their lives over the past century or so to the struggle to save the Indian tiger from extinction, a struggle which then seemed actually to have been won.

But recent events suggest that their battle is by no means over—that, in fact, despite all their efforts, it may already be lost. Project Tiger, the international effort to save the species launched with such high hopes and gaudy fanfare in 1973, and almost universally hailed since as one of the modern conservation movement's greatest success stories, seems likely to have been little more than a momentary delaying action in the species' steady slide toward extinction in the wild.

This is also a more personal book than I had originally intended. I am a biographer and historian, not a biologist or an expert on India or the Indian forests or the great predators that have traditionally ruled them. But I have been visiting and dreaming about those forests for more than four decades now, and the only way I know to convey their special splendor—to suggest what will be lost forever if they disappear from the subcontinent—is simply to describe what I have seen and heard for myself, and I apologize in advance for the number of times the first-person pronoun appears in these pages.

I also apologize if I sometimes sound too relentlessly critical. No one can fault India's resolve to preserve its wildlife; its efforts have outstripped those of any other country in which the beleaguered tiger still finds sanctuary and it has undertaken them in the face of a bewildering array of other challenges. But, since this is a book that deals mostly with what went wrong with Project Tiger, there is comparatively little in its pages about what went right, or about those forest officers who continue, despite everything, to do their jobs with courage and dedication. Without their dogged, unsung work in the field there would long ago have been no tigers or Tiger-Wallahs to write about; without their continuing dedication, the current dispiriting trend can never be reversed.

The reader will necessarily encounter a lot of tigers in this book, but its real subject is the human struggle to save the species. The remarkable men about whom I have chosen to write represent only a handful of those who have become Tiger-Wallahs, but all of them have battled against appalling odds to rescue the tiger and at least a remnant of its wild world, and it is my hope that their personal stories will provide a sort of informal history of the Indian tiger and how it has been treated over the past century. They may seem dissimilar at first: Jim Corbett, the great destroyer of man-eaters who became a still greater conservationist; Billy Arjan Singh, the Spartan farmer who despises hunters and hunting, tried to return a tigress to the wild and, all alone, carved out a national park; Fateh Singh Rathore, the uninhibited Rajput who cheerfully risked his life defending the jungles in his charge; and Valmik Thapar, the son of New Delhi intellectuals, who began as Fateh's disciple, became an authority in his own right, and now champions a new kind of conservation that may provide the tiger's only hope.

But they all share certain qualities—courage, independence and territoriality among them—and all of them are as remarkable in their way as the magnificent animals for whose survival they have risked, and sometimes lost, everything.

I wish I could have written the mostly hopeful book I set out to write. It would be nice to have been able simply to pay tribute to the success of the Tiger-Wallahs I've been lucky enough to know. Instead, my book has become at least in part a record of sights and sounds now not likely ever to be experienced again, a farewell to a world and a species that seem likely to have largely vanished by the century's turn.

The struggle continues. There may still be time to prove my pessimism unfounded. Nothing would please me more.

Geoffrey C. Ward
Maa Farm
Tiger Haven
Manhattan
1983–93

# TIGER-WALLAHS

CHAPTER ONE

# RETURN PASSAGE

Even before I landed again at New Delhi in 1983, it was clear that India had changed. When I was a boy, looking down from one of the prop planes on which my family and I always seemed to come and go after dark, the North Indian landscape below us had been velvety black, featureless. Only the very largest towns were then visible as shimmering pools of light; electricity had not reached far into the countryside, and the winking of the village lamps and cookfires was too faint to be seen from above.

Now, as the big Air India jet began its descent, a brilliant web of light linked the horizons in every direction.

But as soon as my wife Diane and I stepped off the plane into the warm Indian night, my nostrils were filled with the same unmistakable smell of smoke and earth and spice and dung that, even after an absence of three decades, instantly meant India and home to me.

It had not always meant home. I was thirteen in March of 1954, when I first inhaled that rich unsettling aroma, traveling with my father and mother and younger brother and sister, and I had then wanted no part of it. I was born in Ohio and raised on the south side of Chicago, and the most exotic locale I'd seen before we boarded ship for India was Windsor Great Park in England, where we had spent a tranquil, soggy spring two years before. Nor did the notion of anything more exotic have much appeal for me: I had only recently recovered from surgery that had returned my legs to a semblance of normality after polio, and India seemed unimaginably far from the classmates with whom I had been about to enter high school.

But for my father, after too many years of internecine struggle as dean of the college at the University of Chicago, an offer from the Ford Foundation to serve as consultant to the Ministry of Education in New Delhi had proved irresistible. And to my mother, a year or two spent on the opposite side of the globe from Chicago and my father's antagonists—whom she despised with a fervor perhaps only possible for a lapsed Presbyterian—seemed something like a dream.

We traveled to England aboard the S.S. *United States*—first class, because in those days overseas travel was still thought a "hardship," even by the Ford Foundation. When my mother came down with food poisoning the day before we reached Southampton, she felt it was "a judgment," she wrote to her parents. "Here we go to help the poor Indian, stuffing our faces all the way."

We continued to stuff our faces aboard the *Strathmore*, one of the last of the rusty old Pacific & Orient steamers that had ferried the British to and from their imperial holdings since before the turn of the century. The voyage to India took almost three weeks, a mostly uneventful trip enlivened for me when I discovered the ship's library. It was in the charge of a silent, unsmiling Indian steward who kept it suitably ship-shape despite an apparent inability actually to read that had led him to arrange his books—several hundred of them—by color rather than by title.

At the lower left, lined up with military certitude, was a long white and green row of pornographic novels published by the Olympia Press, left aboard at the last

*Opposite*: A tiger in the road at Ranthambhore.

minute by Army officers perhaps, hurrying home after a good time on the continent. I eagerly signed them out, one by one, careful always to conceal them among several more acceptable volumes for my trips to and from the cabin.

Improving literature did not take up all my time, of course. I hurried to the rail to see whales and flying fish and at night leaned over the stern to watch the boiling green and white phosphorescence of the wake, still brooding about home; but my thoughts brightened now and then with secret excitement about what might be in store for us on shore.

Part of that excitement was caused by another book borrowed from the ship's library, *Jungle Lore,* by Colonel Jim Corbett, the intrepid British dispatcher of man-eaters. His accounts of growing up in the Indian forests were irresistible, and I secretly resolved that I would somehow experience as much of this as I could myself.

Perhaps my resolve was not so secret as I like to remember, for shortly after we moved into our house on what were then the outskirts of New Delhi, my father gave me a pellet gun. I began to prowl our compound and the scrub jungle that surrounded it, shooting at the doves that settled on the telephone wires and the little gray-green lizards that skittered along the red-brick garden wall. It was not the killing itself that drew me—though I can't deny that I enjoyed that—so much as the excitement of seeing how close I could get, and the extraordinary sense of power that shooting then represented. It was an activity well outside the tranquil world in which my parents had sought to raise my brother and sister and myself and, perhaps more important, it provided me with vivid proof that even after polio I could affect things directly—even brutally—on my own.

In any case, one Sunday morning two of my father's American friends took me on my first real hunt just a few miles outside the city. They were after antelope. None were to be seen that day, but they lent me an old over-and-under, a combination .22 rifle and .410 shotgun, with which to shoot at anything else that turned up as we drove. I shot a fox, a hare, an owl and a lynx with tufted ears, then took the whole furred and feathered haul home and had myself photographed with it spread out around me on the lawn.

I don't remember my mother's reaction—I suspect she was appalled—but my father seemed delighted. "The boy is a crack shot," he wrote home to my grandparents. "Who would have thought it?" And he paid to have the owl and the lynx stuffed by a local taxidermist. The cat's snarling head hung in my upstairs bedroom until I left India, dust settling on its bright pink tongue.

My parents bought the over-and-under for me, and when it proved too light and too slow to reload for larger game, they gave me a fine old Belgian twelve-gauge shotgun, purchased from two white-bearded Sikhs, proprietors of a gun shop in Connaught Circus that had served the *shikar*—hunting—needs of several generations of British Sahibs. I loved to visit their shop, partly just to admire the polished weapons and boxes of bright red shotgun shells ranked in glass cases around its walls, but also because of the grave courtesy with which its owners treated this fourteen-year-old with round glasses as a mighty hunter.

No gun was ever better cared for than mine, its walnut stock always slippery with oil, its twin barrels gleaming, inside and out. I studied up on wing shooting, doing my best to memorize how-to photo sequences featuring elderly Britons in plaid knickers, then stood in the garden taking pantomime aim at the taunting crows that flapped in and out of our trees.

Despite all my earnest backyard practice, I was never any good at shooting birds. I spent a number of frosty mornings crouched in blinds built in the midst of flooded fields, banging away without success at the ducks and geese that muttered overhead. A slender village boy of twelve or so watched me most of one especially discouraging morning, drawn perhaps by all the noise my friends and I were making, and by the rare spectacle of seeing a wet foreigner so near his home.

"What are you doing, Sahib?" he finally asked after the last birds had moved too far off for us to scare into taking off again. "Do you want ducks? *I* will get them for you. Five rupees." How many did we want?

"Five," I said for no special reason. One number seemed as unlikely as another.

"Wait here," he said. The boy slipped into the water, which just covered his shoulders, and began walking slowly toward the sitting birds.

Big clay water pots bobbed here and there, trapped in the fields when the rains came. He paused to break the neck off one of these, placed its round bottom over his head with just room enough to see, and resumed his slow, steady progress toward the ducks. It took him almost half an hour to reach them. But then, one by one, and with only the slightest disturbance of the surface, he yanked five birds under, holding each there by its feet until it had stopped struggling. The hardest part was bringing them back; his thin legs trembled when he emerged, grinning, from the water, and it took both hands to carry his limp burden. We paid him double what he'd asked. I think that may have been my first faint inkling that there was something inherently silly about shooting.

The four friends who watched with me as the boy drowned ducks that morning were my hunting companions throughout my three and a half years in India. All were much older than I. Bhagat and Harbans Singh were Sikh brothers, descended from a family of hunters, and fine shots. R. V. Raman was an airlines executive for whom Bhagat Singh worked; he was an able, fast-talking, self-made man who seemed to have a hospitable friend or grateful client living near every likely forest and fishing stream in northern India. (Those are not their real names; since my other old friends are still living and I am unclear about the Indian statute of limitations, I have thought it wise to invent new ones for all of them.) The last was my family's Christian driver, Peter John. I suspect that these grown-ups were initially willing to take me hunting mostly because I had access to a jeep, then still a relatively rare thing in India. But after a time they seemed to take a genuine avuncular interest in my having as good a time as they did.

One of Raman's friends was Vikram Singh, the Rao Raja of Alwar, and it was with him that we first hunted in the Sariska forest. He was a chunky little man, soft-spoken and round-faced and almost perpetually melancholy. He was the illegitimate son of the late Maharaja—his title, Rao Raja, was itself a courtly euphemism for "bastard"—and there was a good deal of hard feeling between him and the half brother then on the throne.

Because the boy could never rule, his father had decided when his son was still an infant that something else must be found for him to do with his time. Hunting was the answer, and although the Rao Raja grew wonderfully good at it, I don't think he ever liked it much. From early boyhood on he had been made to stand hip-deep in a nearby lake for hours at a time, firing at wildfowl. When the surface of the lake was at last empty, the birds driven elsewhere, he was still expected to continue shoot-

ing—hundreds, sometimes thousands of shells a day—until his ears rang and his cheek and shoulder were blackened. To teach his son how to bag bigger game on the run, I was told, the Maharaja ordered a railroad track built especially for him up one of the slopes in his state forest and had a flatcar fitted out with stuffed animals—tigers, leopards, an assortment of glassy-eyed deer. A bulletproof cab was constructed for the steam engine that pulled it so that the fireman and engineer could tow the targets up and down the hillside in relative safety. The young Rao Raja fired from a rocky perch across the valley, and when he had riddled all the beasts so that they sagged and spilled out most of their stuffing, replacements were nailed to the flatcar floor and the oversized shooting gallery hauled up the slope again.

The Rao Raja became a superb marksman: without seeming even to aim, he could plink copper *anna* pieces from the sky with a .22 rifle, and by the time I knew him in his mid-thirties, he had accounted for scores of tigers and leopards, hundreds of deer, thousands of birds from his family's preserve. His bravery was celebrated, too: villagers liked to tell of the time he entered a cave alone to track a wounded panther.

It had all bored him. "Too easy," he told me once. "Just bang, bang, bang." Still, he seemed to enjoy driving us into the forest. On the way, as he inched the jeep through the bazaars of his battered old city or slowed to weave through one of the many villages that had once belonged to his father, nothing much seemed to have changed since the old days. Aged men called out greetings to the prince, bowing almost to the ground; at intersections they reached out to touch his feet. Women

Male black buck at the Velavadar Wildlife Sanctuary in Gujarat; once seen everywhere on the Indian plains, these sleek antelope now survive only in a few small and circumscribed herds.

smiled shyly from behind the corners of their saris. Naked children waved. The Rao Raja acknowledged their greetings by lifting one hand slightly from the wheel. At first all this obeisance seemed disturbing to me, but before long I was doing my best to mimic his princely nonchalance.

Despite the reassuring respect shown by his family's former subjects, there was little that was truly princely left to the Rao Raja—except for the spectacular fare said to be prepared in his kitchen. And during my first visit to Alwar, our host promised that the royal cooks would outdo themselves.

That evening, the rich, pungent smells of Indian cooking filled the parlor as I sipped gingerly at a pre-dinner drink, a family specialty brewed in the palace and said to contain the heads of game birds for added zest. (It was bright orange and tasted simultaneously like rosewater and turpentine.) Scores of stylized portraits of the prince's forebears lined the walls, going all the way back to the common ancestor of all Rajput houses, the Sun himself. They all seemed interchangeable to me—each had the same turban, round face, big eyes, flaring mustaches, ropes of pearls—but our host seemed able to tell them apart. A portrait of the radiant founder of his clan hung behind his chair, the family resemblance unmistakable.

As the smell of spices filled the room I could hardly believe my luck. I loved Indian food, but in those days it was very difficult for outsiders to obtain it when dining out. The assumption everywhere seemed to be that we could only survive on the blandest of British fare.

Whether British rule was ultimately good or bad for India is a matter for scholars to decide. But no sane person who ever ate food prepared in the kitchens of the Raj can have any doubts about Britain's culinary legacy: It was universally malign. Never in history has so much bad food been served by so many to so few.

And English food was not only execrable but inescapable. The Sahibs had sailed for home seven years before my family arrived in India, but their death grip on Indian kitchens had not even slightly weakened. Whether you dined at the British-run Hotel Cecil in Old Delhi (where Indians were still discouraged from eating seven *years* after independence), or at Nedou's in the velvet Kashmir Valley of Gulmarg, or at Laurie's in Agra, where dessert was followed by the Taj Mahal by moonlight, the scene and the meal were the same.

There was a big dining room with ceiling fans and dozens of cloth-covered tables, most of them empty. Then as now, India was labor-intensive. One barefoot bearer in starched *pugree* and white uniform gravely showed you to your table. There was a different man to pull out each chair. Another poured the water (which, of course, you dared not drink). Still others brought the food and served it, sometimes four at a time padding around the table, each serving something different from a silver tray. When they were not bringing food or clearing plates, the waiters stood in a solemn line against the wall watching as you worked your way through the courses. You had the sense always that you were silently being measured against the lofty standards of their former masters, and found wanting.

First came the soup—transparent, tasteless, brown, and brought to the table in a big shallow bowl to ensure that it was not only without discernible flavor but cold. A pale cube of carrot floated in it, all alone. This soup was so universally served in India that my brother has suggested it was all prepared in a single cistern somewhere in the Deccan, then piped simultaneously into the kitchens of every club and hotel and rest house catering to foreigners. The subcontinent is the home of mystery,

Male nilghai, or "blue bull," considered sacred by some Hindu villagers because of its presumed resemblance to the cow.

of course, but this theory assumes a brisk efficiency of which India was then, at least, not capable.

The savory followed, a poker chip of toast upon which rested a single warm sardine. Fresh beef was rarely available for the main course for obvious reasons, and water buffalo is an imperfect substitute, so the choice usually came down to mutton (dry and gray and, as often as not, really goat) or roast chicken (pigeon-sized, sinewy and strangled in the kitchen yard that very afternoon). Both came with matching pallid mounds of English "veg" and nicely browned roast potatoes—the best part of the meal, hands-down.

A second savory, often another enshrined sardine, sometimes preceded dessert. Even cooks in very remote outposts could usually manage a good caramel custard, but they too often grew ambitious and proudly offered up instead a big wobbly British "shape," crenellated with cream and identically sweet and tasteless whether tinted pink or green. The peculiar sucking noise the spoon made as it pulled away a serving of this glistening, unsteady favorite remains with me to this day.

At last the Rao Raja's bearer announced that dinner was ready, and we moved into the cavernous dining room and took our places at a long table. A platoon of bearers began filing in through the kitchen door. There must have been twenty steaming dishes. I remember seeing curried partridges and sand grouse and venison. There were hillocks of saffron rice, garnished with raisins and almonds; bowls of golden *dal;* cauliflower and spinach and potatoes and chickpeas with ginger, and all the pickles and chutneys and hot breads that went with them.

My friends dug in. The servants circled wide behind my chair. Then the kitchen door opened again, and the prince paused, a chicken leg halfway to his mouth, and smiled at me. "Cooked *especially* for you," he said, and a beaming servant placed before me another bowl of the universal English soup.

In British times only members of the royal family and their guests had been permitted to shoot at Sariska; the muzzle of anyone else's weapon carried through their land was sealed with wax. But when I hunted there, the forest was at least officially off-limits even to the Rao Raja—though neither he nor the forest officers in charge seemed willing to admit it. He did not slow the jeep at the gatehouse, and the guards in khaki all smiled and saluted as we roared past.

The Rao Raja knew every parched hillside and stony ravine.

"Now," he said, slowing the jeep as we approached a forest curve one afternoon. "Around the corner, in the clearing on your left, you will find seven partridge." We stopped. "Get out, shoot just one, then come right back." I got down and walked up the road, aware that he was waiting, knowing I was supposed to hold up my end, but knowing also that no one, not even the Rao Raja, could possibly know how many birds there would be in an unseen clearing. I saw nothing at first; the clearing seemed empty. But as I stared I began to see them, seven brown-gray birds almost invisible against the brown-gray earth.

I stamped my foot, and when the startled partridges whirred into the air I fired both barrels. Not a feather fell.

"Bad shooting," the prince said as we drove off again.

Most of our hunting at Sariska was done at night, however, and the Rao Raja usually found something else to do just as we were about to set out. I suspect he thought night shooting unsporting but was too polite to say so to his guests. Instead, we were sometimes driven into the dark forest by a local friend of his, a raffish Parsi liquor distributor from Bombay, who owned a sprawling bungalow, a herd of polo ponies and a bright red roofless Buick, built in the 1930s and equipped with twin spotlights powerful enough to transfix any animal we passed. (The car looked a good deal more impressive than it was: Late one afternoon, as we rolled down a steep road, I was startled to see something big and black bounding along ahead of us on the left. It was the rear wheel; seconds later we fetched up against the hillside and had to be towed back to town.) From that Buick's leather-covered back seat one night I fired at a pair of anonymous eyes and killed a chausingha, or four-horned deer, the rarest of all Indian antelope. Since this dainty animal was even then officially protected, I had to leave its small broken body where it had fallen for fear someone would turn us in.

Most of my contacts with the Sariska forest were like that—urgent, ignorant, aimed only at ending lives I did not remotely understand. One favorite road twisted up a stony hillside past several natural pools. A cold mist hung perpetually in this valley on winter nights, and whenever we drove through it we wrapped ourselves in blankets and put up the jeep's windscreen to keep off the chill. A big sambar stag suddenly appeared on the right side of the road one night, his shaggy neck and impressive antlers hung with branches torn from the brush through which he had just come. We stopped. He began to step slowly across the road, head back, one rolling eye glittering in the headlights. I struggled to get to my feet, clawing at the blankets so that I could take aim over the windscreen. My shotgun caught. I fell back. Behind me my friends tried to hold me upright, whispering, "Shoot! Shoot!" Before I could, the stag disappeared down the slope on our left. I dreamed of him for years.

Another night, not far from there, our spotlight picked out a whole constellation of gleaming eyes. Unable to tell stags from does—or even for sure what sort of animals these were—I jumped down to creep closer, careful to keep from being silhouetted in the paralyzing beam. My friends waited in the jeep. I had moved twenty yards or so into the forest when I saw in the topmost branches of the trees the faint shifting glow that meant another car was coming. "Game wardens," I heard Raman say. "Come back!"

Peter called to me: "Hurry up! The patrol is coming." He started the motor. The lights were coming closer, the approaching car's whine now unmistakable. Thorn bushes clawed at my legs. An unseen hole sent me sprawling. "Stay there," Peter hissed. "We'll come back for you."

The jeep roared away. Alone now in the black forest, I could hear the herd moving off through the thickets as the sound of the second car drew nearer. Its lights swung around a curve and the car slid to a stop perhaps twenty feet from where I lay on top of my shotgun. I was certain I was about to be seen, arrested, imprisoned. A spotlight's beam swung over my head, lighting up the thorn bush beneath which I was huddled. A gun barrel slid through the car's front window; two more muzzles appeared at the back. Not game wardens: poachers. Now I would be shot.

I held my breath.

"Nothing. I told you, *nothing*," a voice said from inside the car. "Why don't you listen to me?"

"I'm telling you, something moved in there. I saw it."

More lights appeared in the trees; another motor could be heard. The guns were withdrawn and the car pulled away, splattering me with gravel. I stayed where I

*Pages 8–9:* Tiger on the prowl at Kanha National Park in the central Indian state of Madhya Pradesh.

was. Moments later, my friends drove up. They had circled back for me, and it was their lights that had driven off the strangers.

We spent hour upon hour on those dark roads, peering along the spotlight's beam as it probed and picked its way between the trees and through the grass. Here and there it picked out a remnant of the sanctuary's royal past: gateposts carved with the Alwar coat-of-arms; stone shooting towers; the huge abandoned palace that had once served as the Maharaja's hunting lodge looming white above the undergrowth that choked its abandoned garden.

By three or four in the morning, when every stump in the forest seemed a crouching tiger to our exhausted eyes, we returned to the little Canal Department rest house where we stayed when we were not the Rao Raja's guests. There, the grizzled resident cook would prepare dinner for us—curried venison, if we'd been lucky; chicken otherwise—while we sat on string beds around the fire, talking over the night's hunting. I rarely managed to stay awake long enough to eat, drifting off beneath the stars, surrounded by the fire's warmth and the smell of wood smoke, listening to the distant gunfire that meant other poachers were still out on the road, and to the low sleepy voices of my friends, chuckling at jokes in Hindi I only half understood.

Sometimes the far-off shooting continued all night. It was echoing all over the subcontinent then. Understandably enough, free India's first priority was the growing of enough food to feed its restless, fast-growing population. In the face of that overwhelming need, old forestry practices introduced by the British came to seem somehow undemocratic. Forests were systematically ravaged for timber and fuel, thrown open to graziers, leveled to provide farmers with more land. Gun licenses were issued wholesale for crop protection, an invitation to massive poaching; animals not shot were trapped or poisoned. The export of skins and hides became a major source of foreign exchange. *Shikar* outfitters brought in wealthy foreign sportsmen to mop up what the villagers had overlooked. Demoralized and underpaid officials could earn more by looking the other way than by enforcing wildlife statutes no one bothered about much any more.

Forest cover shrank steadily; wildlife vanished. Even the once-ubiquitous jackals, whose weird cackling yowls had kept us awake in New Delhi itself, were all but annihilated for their skins. The tiger provided the most dramatic evidence of what was happening everywhere. At the turn of the twentieth century, there are said to have been at least forty thousand tigers in India (some authorities put the figure at fifty thousand). By 1972, there were fewer than two thousand, concentrated largely in a few pockets of forest that had once been the exclusive preserves of the Indian princes.

These rulers made implausible conservationists. Their preserves were after all intended primarily to assure them of a steady supply of birds and animals at which to shoot. The sheer volume of game a prince could parade past his guests' guns provided vivid evidence of his wealth and hospitality: the Maharaja of Bharatpur, a small state not far from Sariska, for example, was host to an annual wildfowl shoot; on a single deafening morning in 1938, he and 37 guests (including the British Viceroy, Lord Linlithgow) accounted for 4,327 ducks and geese. Tigers were the top trophy, of course, and the princes vied with one another to see who could run up the highest tally; the hands-down winner was the last Maharaja of Suguja, who claimed 1,150; no other prince ever managed to overtake him—even when some of the overeager among them took to including in their lifetime totals every fetus found in a pregnant tigress.

Still, no one else could shoot in the royal preserves, and so they offered wildlife a kind of qualified but genuine sanctuary rarely found elsewhere. In the early 1970s, as we shall see later, concerned citizens finally forced the Indian government to realize what it had allowed to happen, persuaded it to ban shooting and the export of wild animal skins, and to launch "Project Tiger." As a last-minute effort to rescue the species and something of the complex ecosystem upon which it depended, nine sanctuaries were set aside. Several were former royal preserves but Sariska was not initially one of them—it was not added to the growing roster of Project Tiger Reserves until 1978.

In 1985, I decided to revisit Sariska, to see for myself what had happened to my old hunting grounds in the twenty-eight years since I had last seen them. The dust was the same as it had always been on the old Jaipur road that leads from Delhi to the desert state of Rajasthan. It hung in the hot still air above the field where a farmer and his haggard bullock scratched at the flat, beaten earth; swirled up from the sharp hooves of a herd of goats nibbling their way along the roadside; filtered, gritty, between a traveler's teeth.

But everything else seemed to have changed since, as a boy, I last drove along this road to hunt. Indian wildlife had seemed inexhaustible then. Partridges and peacocks bustled along the shoulders of the road, and the bright green plots of wheat and mustard were home to black buck, so many and so buoyantly curious that at the sight of our jeep rolling along a track then still traveled mostly by bullock carts, they sometimes left off their grazing to race in front of us, scores of them leaping over the road until the dust they kicked up made it impossible to see.

Now, blaring overloaded trucks filled the same road, day and night, and the great bounding herds were gone. I wondered as the familiar landscape flashed by what remained of the animals I had once pursued here with such single-minded enthusiasm.

Since I was a boy, the city of Alwar has become an industrial center, ringed with smokestacks: a billboard on the main road reads "WELCOME TO KELVINATOR COUNTRY." Its feudal past has largely been forgotten, though tourists sometimes visit the florid city palace, and an old bronze cannon still guards a traffic island around which oblivious trucks and motor scooters now flow without a break. The Rao Raja died some years ago, a local man told me; during his last years he had been forced to take a relatively minor bureaucratic job with the democratically elected government he had despised.

But Sariska itself seemed at first unchanged. It remains a parched, inhospitable place, a cluster of sharp quartzite hills and valleys thinly covered with drab forest, relieved only here and there by bursts of brilliant green that signal the presence of a spring or streambed. There is very little rain, and most of what there is falls between July and September; much of the rest of the year the dry leaves of the *dhok* trees that cover all but the steepest slopes are more or less the same dispiriting color as the fine dust thrown into the air at the slightest movement of man or animal. Were the terrain more congenial, of course, the Sariska forest would long ago have been cut and farmed and grazed into oblivion.

The old royal hunting lodge that had been deserted and overgrown in my day

*Pages 12–13:* Nesting storks against the evening sky at the Keoladeo Ghana bird sanctuary near Bharatpur in Rajasthan.

11

had recently been reopened as the Sariska Palace, an aspiring luxury hotel, and painted a gaudy yellow, blue and pink. A bright banner flew again from the central flagstaff—green, red, black and saffron stripes. (Alwar's princely colors, the manager explained, "but rearranged, so no one will accuse us of monarchism.") Inside, the public rooms are oddly gloomy—huge, high-ceilinged, and lit by bare bulbs so feeble that I could see every detail of the glowing filament. The green walls are hung with the white skulls of deer. Tigers in glass cases crouch in the corners; the one next to my table in the dining room was undersized, its stripes faded to tan, its claws rotted away, its tail only recently reattached with plaster.

The lodge is a monument to the turn-of-the-century pretensions of one of India's most bizarre and sinister princes, Maharaja Jay Singh of Alwar. He had persuaded himself that he was the earthly incarnation of the god Rama and was therefore especially rigorous in his orthodoxy: he wore black silk gloves even when shaking hands with the English king, and had two vast towered kitchens, three stories tall, built on either side of his hunting lodge—one for his own food, the other for the preparation of the unclean things his foreign guests insisted on eating. And he was fiercely proud: visiting the Rolls-Royce showroom in London sometime during the 1920s, he asked how much a certain model cost. The salesman smiled; no Indian could possibly afford such a vehicle, he said. Jay Singh ordered ten on the spot, had them shipped home and their roofs torn off; then, to the distress of the Rolls-Royce company and the delight of his fellow princes, sent them out from his city palace each

His Highness Jay Singh of Alwar (leaning on his rifle), a group of British guests, and just part of the army of beaters that drove the striped target past their guns. The Maharaja's hunting reserve is now Sariska National Park in Rajasthan.

morning to collect his subjects' garbage. (The prince could afford such extravagances since, although his state was a comparatively poor one, he routinely appropriated fully half of its revenues for his personal use.)

He privately loathed the British, but always treated those Britons who visited his preserve with distant but elaborate courtesy. Goats were tied atop a table in the center of the walled garden and its gate was left open so that leopards would get used to padding past the lawn furniture in search of easy meals; the moonlit after-dinner kills are said to have delighted the ladies seated on the verandah. His entire state army was routinely marshaled to beat the Sariska forests for his guests, squads of infantry and cavalry and an elephant corps driving before them everything that walked or flew. The shooting towers I had seen as a boy were his, too: tall, thick-walled, and provided with cushions and gun slits so that visitors could safely sit and sip their whiskey-sodas while waiting for a tiger to kill the plaintive buffalo calf tethered to an iron ring just a few steps away.

When no visitors were about, Jay Singh's private life was filled with cruelty. It amused him to stake out elderly women and small children as bait. He was said to be given to sexual excesses with small boys, as well as with the young women his agents routinely kidnapped off the streets of his city. Evenings in his private chambers were even said sometimes to end in murder. The British did nothing about any of this—Sir Edwin Montague, the Secretary of State for India, is said to have specially admired Jay Singh's unfailing good manners—but in 1933 the Maharaja went too far. After his polo pony threw him during a hotly contested chukkar, he doused it with gasoline and set it ablaze. At that, the animal-loving British exiled him forever from his state.

Under Project Tiger, access to Jay Singh's forests was at least officially controlled. No visitor could enter the reserve without a forest guard to serve as guide.

Ramchandran Singh was my guide, a slender young man with a waxed mustache and blinding teeth. Beyond the gate, the scrub forest still spread out on either side of the narrow tarmac that ran between the brown hills, just as I remembered, and within a hundred yards I spotted two nilghai moving through the roadside brush on our left. My friends and I had shot a good many of these big antelope whose fancied resemblance to cattle makes some Hindus revere them as sacred; their meat was in fact a fair substitute for beef and filled the freezers of a good many foreigners in New Dehli. They are ungainly, even ludicrous animals—the slate gray males have white-striped ankles and a ragged goatee and are built on a sort of slant—but it was wonderful to see them again, and so close to the road. What good luck, I thought, and clapped Ramchandran on the shoulder.

He seemed a little startled at my enthusiasm. We would see many more, he assured me. I thought he was being overly optimistic. I knew this place, after all; one or two brief glimpses like this were all one could expect. But within half a mile or so, we were surrounded by hundreds of antelope and deer grazing in the feathery grass or filing to one or another of the seven artificial water holes that lined the road.

There were nilghai and sambar in groups of five and six, and chital—the spotted deer that are among the most beautiful on earth—in herds of ten to twenty. There had been no chital at all when I hunted at Sariska. Now they seemed to be everywhere—some six thousand of them, if the field director's census figures were correct—all descended from three or four terrified animals chased here by dogs when a royal deer park nearby was obliterated not long after I left India in 1957. And I had never before seen sambar in the daytime—there were now said to be six thousand of *them*.

For someone who remembered this place as dark and mysterious, its animals as furtive, even ghostly, Sariska now seemed a revelation. It was the end of the mating season, Ramchandran told me. Chital fawns minced through the grass. A sambar stag, even larger than the one of which I sometimes still dreamed, lowered his great head and horns and sprayed himself spectacularly with urine; the smell, Ramchandran assured me, would make him irresistible to the does that waited a few yards away. Here and there among the trees, young chital stags clashed with elaborate ceremony: heads down, antlers locked, feet braced, they strained back and forth, whining with the effort like big angry babies; then they simultaneously lifted their heads, froze to glare into one another's eyes from a distance of perhaps two feet, and went back at it.

It was all almost too much. I had a sense after a while that I was in some sort of safari park, that the herds must be only half wild—a feeling that intensified when the animals hardly flinched as a brightly painted tour bus hurtled past us, its passengers leaning out the windows to hoot at them.

An afternoon in a small cinder-block blind on the edge of a waterhole changed my mind. Lying on a mattress in the dark, cool interior of the hide, just thirty feet from the furthest edge of a muddy pool, I found myself in the midst of a steady, slow-moving procession of thirsty animals whose every waking moment seemed spent in terror—not of the people passing by in vehicles, who no longer represent a menace to them, but of the unseen tiger that can lie hidden anywhere. The deer and the antelope approached the water with infinite wariness, nostrils flaring to catch the faintest scent, ears alert for telltale sounds, big eyes wide and staring, placing their hooves gingerly, as if they feared the earth itself might suddenly move beneath them.

The delicate four-horned antelope that drink near noon seemed most skittish; it took each one two or three tries to work up the courage actually to approach the pool, and once they had swallowed their precious mouthful of water, they raced back to the woods in frenzied bounds. But the larger animals were only slightly less tentative. Later that afternoon, ten chital were bunched along one side of the pool and a big sambar stag was approaching slowly, ready to join a pair of does already at the water, when two baby wild boar ran into the clearing, all head and very little body, kicking up with their frantic trotters two tiny busy clouds of dust. The stag bellowed as if two tigers were charging and galloped toward the forest; his does beat him to the treeline. The chital had already vanished. With the big clearing all to themselves, the piglets raced back and forth in perfect tandem for perhaps three minutes before drinking and rushing off again.

I witnessed more forest life in that single afternoon than I'd seen during three and a half years of hunting. A big nilghai stalked down to the water, his striped ankles especially clownish seen close up, the insides of his enormous twitching ears glowing pink before he dipped his head. A chital stag slipped up behind him and, although there was plenty of room, jolted him hard in the backside with his antlers. The startled nilghai, far larger than his tormentor but equipped with horns no longer than my index finger, trotted hastily away. The deers' antlers reached extraordinary size now that hunting had ended: one old chital, his blunt muzzle gray with age, bore horns so huge and heavy that it seemed miraculous that he could hold them upright, let alone move between the trees of the forest without help.

The sounds of the forest were new to me, too. One after another, all afternoon, the far-off chital stags challenged one another, their horny wheezes echoing from the slopes, and when a band of perhaps twenty nervous young chital shouldered their way to the edge of the pond, they kept up a high-pitched running commentary of squeals and whines, as if to reassure one another that it was really all right to take a moment out from their eternal vigilance to drink. A few moments later, five peafowl waddled down to the water. While the hens drank, the lone male began his courting dance, his huge fan spread out above him. When that iridescent spectacle failed to impress one thirsty hen, he stood stock-still behind her and began literally to vibrate with longing, his clashing feathers producing an astonishingly loud chatter which certainly impressed me—though the hen for which it was intended remained unmoved.

No tiger came to the pool while I was there. I had never seen one at Sariska in the old days, either. (Once, I thought I had, at night; I took aim at its striped haunch, then held my fire, hoping the half-hidden animal would move and offer me a clearer shot. It did. It was a hyena.)

After dark that first evening, and for three evenings after that, Ramchandran tried very hard to show me a tiger. He drove with me up and down the dark roads I remembered so well, holding a spotlight out the window and swinging its white beam furiously from one side of the road to the other so as not to leave a yard of forest unexamined.

"Sambar," he would whisper, able instantly to see the whole outline of an animal whose gleaming eyes were all I had time to glimpse, then whirl to catch a chital as it faded into the brush on the opposite side. Several porcupines rattled across the road; a civet tumbled after one of them, a white ball in the headlights, its striped tail stretched out behind it like a pennant.

But no tiger ever appeared. "One thing certain," Ramchandran muttered to the driver. "VIPs *never* see a tiger."

Before heading back to the hotel for the last time, we stopped at a guard post deep in the sanctuary. It was cold, and the five forest guards who lived there made room for us around their fire. One poured me a cup of spiced tea. I was sorry at having failed again to see a tiger where I had always hoped to see one. Perhaps I would do better at the Ranthambhore Tiger Reserve, the next stop on my trip. But as I sipped the tea my disappointment was swept away by memory. Everything came back to me from thirty years before: the velvet black of the surrounding hills against the star-filled sky; the low voices of my companions; the smell and welcome warmth of the fire. There was no distant shooting now. It had been replaced by a new and comforting sound: from just beyond the firelight came the strenuous clacking of two chital stags, contesting to ensure the future of their herd.

When I told Ramchandran that we were on our way to Ranthambhore National Park with an introduction to its field director, Fateh Singh Rathore, he was clearly impressed. "A *very* dangerous man," he said, by which I think he meant that Fateh Singh was brave and resolute. He was in fact a legend among Indian conservationists: no wildlife official had worked harder or sacrificed more to protect the land and animals under his care; none had seen his hard work crowned with greater success.

Under his implacable protection, the number of tigers flourishing at Ranthambhore had grown from thirteen to forty in just thirteen years. "You will see a tiger at Ranthambhore," Ramchandran assured me as I left Sariska. "Fateh Singh can *always* show you one."

Ranthambhore, located at the junction of two ranges of red hills, the Vinidhyas and Aravaillis, is no more lush than Sariska: neon parakeets and iridescent bee-eaters provide the brightest spots of green among its seared hillsides. But it is far more beautiful. The towers and sprawling battlements of a vast, abandoned tenth-century fortress cover the top of its highest hill; for centuries, Ranthambore was the hunting preserve of the princes of Jaipur, and scattered all through its forests are crumbling walls, fallen temples, and carved *chatris*—domed monuments, each marking the spot where some long-forgotten man of consequence was cremated.

A chain of three small, bright blue lakes runs down the center of the preserve, and Diane and I stayed for several days on the shore of the largest of these, in a restored pavilion that was once the home of a holy man and therefore called the Jogi Mahal. From its cool verandah I watched crocodiles and soft-shelled turtles sun themselves and herds of chital browse along the shore. Sambar came down to the water, too, and splashed right in to stay for hours, immersed among succulent lotus pads, their broad backs becoming islands for snowy egrets.

This extraordinary place was Fateh Singh's domain. He is a Rathore, a member of the ancient princely family of Jodhpur. He has none of his ancestors' bloody-mindedness, but he has inherited their fascination with the forest and their sense of proprietorship over everything that lives within it. To this day he speaks of Ranthambhore as "my park," its tigers as "my tigers"; and during our first visit with him, both did still seem to be his and his alone.

He was in his mid-forties then, short and chesty, with a steel gray mustache, and given to sporty hats, sunglasses, and dapper green safari clothes. There was little of the ascetic about him: he savored a bawdy joke and a stiff drink on the rooftop of his forest home after dark, and he let nothing interfere with his favorite situation comedy in Hindi, watched on a small black-and-white set powered by a car battery. But his animals came first, always; everything about them seemed to interest him.

"There's your music!" he shouted, as we drank a cup of tea shortly after dawn on our first morning at Ranthambhore. We were listening to the steady *poot-poot-poot* of the coppersmith which, he said, meant that summer was coming fast. The forest chorus grew more complex, a discordant blending of the shrill triple-noted call of the gray partridge; the peacock's contralto *peeaor;* the insistent "Did-you-do-it? Did-you-do-it?" of the lapwing; finally, the gray langur monkeys' deep solemn hooting. "They're telling each other, 'I'm okay, you're okay,'" Fateh said. "Glad they got through another night."

Suddenly the langurs' mellow conversation turned to angry, hawking coughs. We put down our teacups and raced for Fateh's jeep. From their perches in the tops of trees, langurs are often the first to announce the presence of a prowling tiger. We would spend the next four days like firefighters, careening over the stony landscape to answer every alarm. As we drove, Fateh sat ramrod-stiff in the back, humming to himself at the sheer pleasure of being in his forest, and occasionally pointing out one or another of the 275 species of birds seen here.

Despite Ramchandran's confidence in him and Fateh Singh's intimate knowledge of the Ranthambore tigers (half of which he knew by name and could identify at a glance), even he could not summon up a tiger to show visitors at will. We drove through his preserve for four days, off and on, listening for the alarm calls of deer and monkeys, and leaning down from time to time to examine the pug marks of tigers that seemed always to have just preceded us on the twisting forest track.

In the late afternoons we parked overlooking one or another of the lakes, hoping to see a tiger charge out of the grass to kill one of the hundreds of deer feeding there. One evening as we sat watching in the fading golden light, we suddenly spotted two figures strolling along the path toward us: a tall Englishman hung with binoculars and wearing khaki shorts, arm-in-arm with an eighty-year-old Dutch woman whom I recognized as a fellow guest at the Jogi Mahal. Just three days earlier, news had reached Ranthambhore that a tiger had killed another heedless Briton who had insisted on entering the forest on foot to get a closer look at a rare species of owl in the Corbett Tiger Reserve more than two days' drive to the north. Now this mismatched, oblivious couple had dawdled along for hundreds of yards between high yellow walls of grass whose soft sibilance in even a faint breeze can disguise the movements of the clumsiest tiger. Fateh was apoplectic. "Stupid! Stupid! Bloody idiots!" he shouted at the startled visitors, pulling them into his jeep. "I should throw you out of this park. You will get my tigers killed!"

People, not animals, remained his most vexing problem. In the heart of the Ranthambhore fortress is a temple dedicated to Ganesha, the fat, amiable, elephant-headed god who blesses all new ventures, including marriage and childbearing. Small groups of worshippers seeking his favor climb the hill every morning, and on one annual festival day some fifty thousand pilgrims troop along the main sanctuary

Gray langurs, scattered across a Ranthambhore slope, rely on the sentinel at the upper right to scan the valley floor for predators.

*Pages 20–21:* A herd of sambar keeps anxious watch as a patrolling tigress passes along the shore of the Rajbagh lake at Ranthambhore.

road to converge on the temple. Even Fateh Singh did not dare interfere with the rights of the faithful to worship where they please, but he did worry about what might happen if one of his tigers should someday attack a pilgrim. (On the same festival day in 1988, Fateh's worst fears were confirmed. A young tigress which had been prevented from crossing the road for hours by the parade of pilgrims streaming past without a break finally lashed out and killed a seven-year-old boy whose father had left him for a moment to relieve himself.)

Then, too, scattered among the deepest ravines, lived a handful of solitary *sadhus*—ascetic hermits who had vowed to end their days there, praying in the wilderness. Fateh wasn't sure how many there were—perhaps five, he said—and, so far, the animals had left them alone. The sadhus attributed this to the power of their own belief; Fateh credited "damned good luck."

He did the best he could to control the rest of those who sought admission to his sanctuary. No one was allowed to walk in the forest; tourists had to be driven by trained guards, and a good deal of his time was spent allocating seats for them among the small fleet of spavined vehicles at his disposal. One evening I counted thirty-nine spectators packed into five parked jeeps, all of us watching to see if a single noisy sambar calf would find its missing mother before a hungry predator found it. (It did.)

The most serious trouble came from local people. A dozen villages had been successfully shifted out of the park, but thirty more ringed its perimeter; its trees had always provided fuel for their cookfires; its grass and undergrowth had fed their herds; and the villagers were only bewildered and angered by the notion that the forest should suddenly be off-limits to them. Women slipped into the park through hidden ravines to cut the grass, carrying out great heaps of it on their heads. Troops of woodcutters entered, too, and so did herdsmen, and tribal hunters with packs of trained dogs.

Fateh Singh and his forest guards did their best to fend them all off, but it was not easy. He had too few men to patrol the entire border of the park. The grasscutters hid their curved blades beneath their skirts, then charged the guards with molestation when they were searched. When disputes arose, local politicians routinely favored the villagers—who can vote—over animals that cannot.

One morning during our visit a forest guard staggered into the field director's office, the side of his face bruised and badly swollen. He had been beaten by four woodcutters. Fateh Singh instantly dispatched a party of his own men to retaliate in kind. "We can't treat these people the way you do in America," he said. "No psychiatrists here. We don't ask, '*Why* do you do this?' We just give them a good bashing."

He was a stern sovereign, but he tried hard to be fair. When the former Maharani of Jaipur visited her family's old hunting lodge just outside the park and ordered that several partridges be shot for her guests' luncheon, Fateh Singh took her to court. "There must be the same law for rich and poor," he told me. The Maharani's case was just one of some three hundred he then had pending in the Indian courts.

His was an intensely personal struggle. Whenever he left his stronghold even for a few days, interlopers streamed across its borders and had to be driven out again when he got back. "It's an endless war," he told me as we drove through the forest on my last morning at Ranthambhore, and it was one he would have preferred not to have to fight. Despite almost daily threats and his own near-fatal beating, he refused

A submerged sambar
stag dines on lotus leaves
at Ranthambhore.

to carry a gun—and wouldn't let his men carry them, either. "I'm too hot-tempered," he told me. "If I had a gun I know I would shoot someone." Besides, "we want to be friendly, to work *with* the people, not against them. What we need is a 'Project People for Project Tiger.'" He called for teams of conservation workers to move from village to village, explaining the long-term benefits of keeping the forests intact; a program to recruit tribal hunters into the forest service so that their forest skills could be used to save animals rather than slaughter them. The periphery of the park should be replanted with improved grasses for harvesting, he said, but only to nourish stall-fed livestock—and funds had to be found to encourage traditional herdsmen to abandon their inferior, wasteful animals in favor of improved breeds. All of this would take time and money and coordinated planning.

In the meantime, the tigers of Ranthambhore had only Fateh Singh. He had worked within the sanctuary for nearly twenty years, and his success had several times led his superiors at Jaipur to promote him to a desk job. He always turned them down. He planned to stay in one place—and in charge—until he retired. "I know this place," he explained, rising in his seat to peek over the top of the thorn bushes. "I'm not happy anywhere else. I've bought myself a farm at the edge of the forest so that every day until I die I can drive over and visit my park."

He clutched my shoulder. "Tiger in the road," he said. Perhaps forty feet ahead of us a tiger sat in the middle of the track—filled the track, in fact, and seemed somehow to fill the forest that stretched away on either side as well. Nothing had prepared me for his size or for the palpable sense of menace and power that emanated

from him. "His name is Akbar," Fateh whispered, beginning softly to hum with pleasure at the sight of him. "About five hundred pounds."

The tiger rose slowly to his feet. Everything about him seemed outsized: his big, round, ruffed face; his massive shoulders and blazing coat; his empty belly that hung in folds and had finally forced him into the open to hunt; his long twitching tail. It seemed inconceivable that such a big vivid animal could have stayed hidden in this drab open forest for so long.

We sat very still in the open jeep as the tiger stared at us. "He's a good boy," Fateh said, still humming. I devoutly hoped so. The tiger turned and cocked his huge head to listen as a sambar called from a clearing off to our left; then, after fixing us with one more steady glance, he slipped silently into the grass. Neither his smiling protector nor his protector's wary guests had been worth so much as a growl.

I had only dreamed of tigers as a boy. Black buck were what I really hunted, fleet delicate antelope whose spiraling horns and richly patterned skins made handsome trophies. They had been scattered nearly everywhere across the North Indian plains then, as I have said, and my friends and I had traveled nearly everywhere in search of them.

I knew them only as targets, of course. Sometimes Bhagat Singh shot them with his old rifle from what always seemed to me to be fantastic distances. Much more often, we pursued them in our jeep, Peter at the wheel, careening around thorn bushes at

One of Ranthambhore's abandoned pavilions offers shelter to a tiger.

24

forty miles an hour, slamming across rutted fields, flying over the tamped mud walls that separated one man's crop from the next, while my friends and I struggled both to stay in our seats and to fire buckshot into the frantic zigzagging animals ahead of us. Once, our jeep turned entirely over, though with such merciful slowness that we were all able to step safely out into the soft dust; an amused old farmer and his bullocks came along and helped us to right ourselves. At harvest time we had to be particularly careful not to hit the village women hidden, kneeling, in the billowing wheat.

I must have shot thirty black buck during my years in India. At the end of one especially busy day, my friends and I drove home with thirteen of them heaped beneath a flapping tarpaulin in the back of our jeep, enough to fill my family's freezer and those of our friends for several months. I could sense always that my parents were of two minds about my shooting; they liked having the fresh meat and they thought it good that I had a hobby that got me out of the house and into the outdoors. But I think they also found all the apparently gleeful killing a little alarming, and I was always vague about the dangers of our hunts for fear my parents might have second thoughts about letting me go. I know my mother worried anyway, and sometimes took to her bed until I got back safely, and once or twice my father asked to accompany me, not because he had any interest in shooting, I suspect, but because he thought my mother would feel better if he came along.

Two American agricultural advisors took us out with them one morning. They were country boys, one thin, the other fat, and they couldn't get over their good luck in having been stationed in a country where hunting was so easy and hunting laws were so lax. We drove out to a series of stony hills just a few miles from Delhi. I had my shotgun. The fat hunter lent my father a spare rifle, a 30.06 with a telescopic sight. We shot a partridge or two shortly after sunup, but saw nothing else worth shooting until midmorning, when a placid nilghai appeared suddenly at the foot of a scrub-covered hill just off the road. The two hunters urged my father to take a shot at him; he was barely fifty yards away, a big animal, and standing broadside to us. Hard to miss. But my father was as nearsighted then as I am now, and could not make him out against the hillside. The watery magnified image in the scope did not help. "Shoot before he runs," the fat hunter urged. The muzzle moved helplessly over the slope. Finally, just to please the rest of us, I think, my father pulled the trigger. Dust exploded from the hillside, yards above the nilghai but close enough to send him lumbering out of sight. I was embarrassed by my father: How could he not even have *seen* him?

A little later, we saw a black buck feeding in a mustard field. It was the fat man's turn. He turned off the engine, cradled the rifle on his knee and took a long time aiming. At the sound of the rifle, the buck staggered and fell. We drove close and got down, my father still carrying the borrowed rifle.

The buck was trying to get up, to get away. Its back legs scrabbled for purchase, but its front legs were useless; the fat man's bullet had smashed through both shoulders.

The thin man offered his congratulations. The fat one thanked him. They agreed the horns weren't bad. Not great, but not bad.

The buck watched us, mouth open, snorting flecks of blood. More blood was pooling in the dust. Maybe he'd be worth taking to the taxidermist, the thin one suggested.

The buck began a low, shuddering bawling, its eyes rolling. It tossed its head and horns from side to side. But which taxidermist? There were two in Delhi, one a good deal more expensive than the other, but also more artistic.

Gripping the barrel of the rifle with both hands, my father brought the stock down onto the buck's skull. The animal kicked more urgently. He swung the rifle again high above his head this time, then down as hard as he could. The buck stiffened, then relaxed. The terrible bawling stopped, but the rifle stock had splintered.

The hunters were polite but full of scorn. The buck had really been dead, they said: it couldn't feel anything. They would have gotten around to cutting its throat. Besides, the stock had been expensive and would be hard to replace.

As we picked up the dead buck and swung it by its frail legs into the back of the jeep, my father offered to pay whatever it took to have the rifle repaired. I didn't know what to say to him on the long drive home, but I knew inside myself that he had done what I should have done: that what my friends and I had been doing was wrong.

Not long after that trip I left India with my family. The killing of the black buck continued. By 1970, only a few scattered herds survived outside the sanctuaries.

The largest concentration of them, however—some twelve thousand animals, I was told—now lived near Jodhpur, not under the protection of the Rajasthan State Forest Department but as the fiercely defended charges of a small Hindu sect called the Bishnois, whose fields and villages encircle that medieval desert city. The Bishnois followed the teachings of a fifteenth-century Hindu guru they call Jambaji. There were twenty-nine principles to his creed—the sect's name derives from the Hindi words for twenty and nine, *bis* and *no*—and they included tenets common to ascetics everywhere: no tobacco or alcohol, no cursing or lies or impure foods. But two of his teachings were unique: All animals were to be considered sacred, but the black buck was the most sacred of all; anyone who dared hunt them on Bishnoi lands did so at his peril. And because green trees offered the antelope shelter from the desert sun, they must never be cut down.

The Bishnois' devotion has rarely been found wanting. When an eighteenth century ruler of Jodhpur sent his army to fell a number of feathery *khedaji* trees to make way for a royal thoroughfare to his city, the Bishnoi women are said to have barred its way, embracing the trees and warning that they were willing to die rather than have them destroyed. Three hundred and sixty-three Bishnois, most of them women, were killed, along with the trees to which they clung. It is the Bishnoi women who still sacrifice most for the welfare of the herds; tradition requires that for every four pots of precious water they carry home to their families, a fifth must be brought to fill the communal trough from which the wild antelope drink on summer evenings, and it is the women who make sure that each village maintains its store of hoarded grain which sustains the antelope in lean times. But at the sound of a shot, it is the men who come running; suspected poachers are seized, bound to trees, and beaten senseless. Some years back an unwitting wildlife photographer had to be rescued after he was found focusing what seemed to the Bishnois to be a suspiciously long telephoto lens.

At Jodhpur, I was told to call upon a prince of the former royal family, a hunter-turned-conservationist, my informant assured me, who would be eager to introduce me to the Bishnois and to show me the herds that thrive under their protection. He turned out to be a bald, sinewy little man with a flaring Rajput mustache, whose brisk hauteur perfectly suited his new status as a hotelkeeper. He seemed remarkably uninterested in my plans to write about the wildlife of his district until I suggested that I would be happy to pay him for his trouble. At that he brightened a little: although he was preparing for the wedding of his daughter, he told me, he would be willing to take the time to drive me out into the countryside for the equivalent in rupees of fifty dollars. And he knew where there was a rare white buck; if he managed to show it to me, I was to give him an additional "present." I agreed.

The prince—I think it best not to give his name in light of what happened later—picked me up in his jeep the following morning. He was a taciturn, even sullen guide at first, answering my questions in grunts and monosyllables as he gripped the wheel. No admiring words I could summon up to say about the flat, shriveled landscape around his city seemed to make him brighten, and after twenty mostly silent minutes we turned off the main road and onto the first of a series of rutted, dusty village tracks. Neither they nor his jeep had improved since it was built in 1942, and conversation grew still more difficult as I tried to stay in my seat.

I did manage to ask about the Bishnois: Was it true that they still protected the herds? "Yes, yes, of course they do," he said, scowling, "though the women are too lazy to bring as much water for them as they once did." But the old story that his royal ancestors had "cut down the bloody trees and the bloody girls with them" was a lie, invented during the struggle for Indian independence by Congress Party politicians who wanted to make the princes look bad in retrospect. He knew politicians, he added; he had himself represented the district in the legislative assembly: "My people love me." Certainly they were deferential. When we stopped for a cup of tea, the villagers crowded around our jeep, the men in big loose turbans and wearing locket portraits of Guru Jambaji, the women dressed in burnished reds and oranges, their thin wrists and ankles heavy with hammered silver. When I asked them what they would do if they saw someone with a gun near their village, the men all laughed and chopped at their necks with the side of their right hands as a sign of how severely he would be dealt with.

We began to see animals as soon as we left their village. Nilghai trotted heavily away as we clanked through an arid, unplanted area, and delicate chinkara gazelles stopped nibbling at isolated thorn bushes to watch us pass, their edginess betrayed only by the agitated waggling of their downturned tails.

And when we came out into the green open fields again, I felt as if I were back in the midst of some boyhood dream. Black buck were everywhere, hundreds of them, chasing one another through the crops, jousting with their spiral horns, dancing right up to the mud walls of the Bishnoi villages. Farmers on camels moved placidly among them; so did bullock carts heaped with fodder and village women carrying water on their heads.

The prince barely slowed. There was no sense in stopping: there were always plenty more animals to see as we circled his city, and besides, he wanted to find the rare white buck that would earn him his additional payment.

I was astonished, and in my astonishment began to tell him of my past, of how many of these animals I had killed, of how wonderful it was to see them again.

"*See* them? What's the use of *seeing* them?" he said, suddenly alert and enthusiastic. "You're a hunter, you say. So am I. Don't you want to *shoot* them?"

Surely shooting was impossible, I said, a thing of the past.

"Difficult but not impossible," the prince said, taking my surprise for encouragement and warming to his topic. Laws were made to be broken. True, it would be hard to shoot here. Too open, he said; though he could hit a buck with the jeep if I liked: "No noise."

Of course it would cost me. He could arrange a hunt in one of his family's old sanctuaries some distance from Jodhpur, he said, gesturing vaguely toward the faint blue hills that lined the horizon. A relation lived there who was in charge of such things.

What would I like to shoot? A crocodile? A sloth bear? A panther? Sadly, there were no tigers in his lands any more, but anything else was possible for the right price. We would shoot with a spotlight at night, of course. Five hundred dollars and a few bottles of imported liquor would cover everything, including something for his relative and payments to the local villagers for their silence. For a little more he could have the skins and heads prepared for me, though I would have to have them smuggled out of India on my own. That should not be a problem, he added; his friends at the Delhi embassies used their diplomatic pouches.

A chinkara buck gazed at us from behind a bush just off the road. The prince stopped the jeep. "He would not dare stick his head up like that if I had a two-two," he said, taking imaginary aim. "When you come you must bring me one, and plenty of ammunition. And maybe a silencer as well." All I needed to do, his words tumbling now as we drove on, was to send him a telegram saying I was arriving for "the party." We would both know what that meant, and he would have everything ready when he met me at the Jodhpur airport.

It was hot and still now, nearing noon, and the antelope had begun to cluster in the shade of the scattered trees.

"There he is," the prince said, wrenching the jeep off the track and into the fields. The white buck lay alongside two normally colored ones beneath a *khedaji* tree. His fragile legs were folded decorously beneath him and his horns seemed unusually long. We picked up speed as we rattled through the newly planted mustard. All three animals rose to their feet, staring at the oncoming jeep. Then they began to skip forward, to run, finally to bound, racing across the fields at right angles to us, making for a high mud wall overgrown with thorns.

We swerved to follow and drove faster. I held on with both hands. The white buck lagged a little behind the others. His left hind leg seemed to have been injured.

"Some village dog's been at him," the prince shouted, as the jeep rose in the air and slammed down again. "Damn it, I knew I should have shot him when I last had the chance. Now someone else will get him." He gunned the motor.

The other two bucks did not even pause at the wall, soaring over it in the sure knowledge that we could never follow. The white buck slowed, then scrambled to his left, head down, horns held flat against his back, running along the wall looking for an opening.

We roared closer.

He stumbled, then gathered himself and leaped over the wall, white against the blue sky, floating, already almost like a ghost.

## CHAPTER TWO
# A TIGERCIDAL THIRST

My experience with the bloody-minded prince had not been encouraging. Clearly, the survival of Indian wildlife was still a fragile business. But the apparent health of Sariska, the wonders of Ranthambhore and the example set there by Fateh Singh Rathore seemed to me to be evidence that all was not lost, that despite the odds the forests I had so loved as a boy and now had come to love again had a real chance of surviving.

At least once a year over the course of the last ten, I have managed to make it back to the jungles, usually on assignment for one American magazine or another, but when I could not manage that, on my own.

During most of those trips Diane and I were lucky enough to hire the same driver, a small, courtly man named Shadi Ram Sharma, whose inbred calm behind the wheel is a great comfort on India's frenetic roads, statistically the most dangerous on earth. Having spent hundreds of hours together, racketing across North India, we have become friends. In 1985, when Diane and I planned to spend a week at Tiger Haven, the home of Billy Arjan Singh (one of the Tiger-Wallahs the reader will get to know later in this book), on the edge of Dudhwa National Park, we asked him to bring along his wife Shashi and their two sons.

As a boy, Shadi Ram had glimpsed a little of India's wildlife. He had been born in a village north of Delhi in the 1950s, and remembered vividly the antelope and wild boar that still lived along the Jumna River then, and he dimly recalled hearing as a small child that a leopard had taken a goat from its thorn enclosure in the heart of his village. He still lives in that village, but it has long since been swallowed up by Delhi's relentless sprawl. The green fields of wheat and mustard that once surrounded it are gone now, obliterated by a tangle of filth-strewn streets, crowded bazaars and workers' colonies hung with washing. Neither his wife nor their boys had ever so much as seen a wild animal, and we had brought them along with us this time hoping that while we were visiting Billy and his family, they might drive through the park and experience at least something of the jungle. The grasslands that once spread southward from the Himalayan foothills and surrounded Dudhwa were among the richest wildlife areas in India in the old days, and the beleaguered park still offers the visitor at least a hint of what the Indian forests once were. Perhaps, we hoped, Shadi Ram and his family would even be lucky enough to see a tiger.

Shashi did not share our hope. The closest she had ever come to a tiger was the gaudy calendar on her wall on which the warrior-goddess Durga is depicted riding one, and she had been steeped since girlhood in superstitious tales of tigers that stalk men and gulp their blood, and possess great and malevolent powers over anyone who happens upon them. She was frankly terrified by the prospect even of entering the forest.

Her husband had insisted that she come anyway, and not long after the white Ambassador entered the park and turned onto one of the ancient logging roads that run between tall stands of teak, he later told me, a massive male tiger emerged from the undergrowth on the left, stood and stared for a moment at the oncoming car, then eased himself down in the center of the road and sat there, motionless, but for the steady twitching of its tail.

Shashi let out a muffled scream. The boys in the back seat shouted. Their father shushed them, stopped the car, and turned off the motor.

They sat stone-still.

The tiger continued to stare.

Shashi closed her eyes, lifted her folded hands to her forehead in supplication, and began to pray to Durga. "Oh, Goddess, the tiger is your vehicle," she said. "Please, remove it from the road."

After a moment, the tiger rose, stretched, and, still looking back, stalked off into the undergrowth.

Durga embodies the power of good over evil above all her other attributes, and it seems fitting that the tiger should be her emblem. For it is power—awesome but contained—that the tiger seems to embody, in nature as well as Hindu mythology.

The tiger is an immigrant to India. The latest evidence seems to suggest that the species was born in China, not Russia as had previously been assumed, and spread outward from there, west to Turkey, east as far as Siberia, and southward into the Indian subcontinent. Until this century there were eight subspecies. Three—the Caspian, Javan and Balinese tigers—are already extinct. The other five—the Siberian, Chinese, Indo-Chinese, Sumatran and the Indian—are all in grave danger.

The Indian subspecies—the Bengal tiger, or *panthera tigris tigris*—is still thought to be the most numerous; though, as we shall see, accurate numbers are hard to come by. The tiger once ruled most of the subcontinent, from the dry scrub forests of what is now the desert states of Rajasthan in India all the way east to the tangled mangrove swamps of the Sundarbans that now form India's border with Bangladesh, and from the wooded slopes of the Himalayan foothills all the way south to the deep green jungles of the Indian states of Karnataka and Tamil Nadu.

And, although the tiger's range has been reduced with dizzying speed in recent years, locking him up within a few scattered pockets of forest, his suzerainty has never been entirely forgotten. The tiger continues stubbornly to haunt the imaginations of the millions of men, women, and children whose sheer profusion seems likely to spell his doom. He still appears everywhere—on calendars and T-shirts, in poetry and folk dances, daubed in white on village walls made of mud, menacing the hero in gaudy Bombay films.

The earliest Indian representations of tigers are found carved on Harappan seals, dating from about 2300 B.C. At least one shows a man up a tree at whose foot stands a tiger. Some writers have suggested that the tiger has simply treed the man (who does look distinctly unhappy). Others believe the tableau is meant to show that both man and tree—and, by extension, all of nature—owe their existence to the life force the tiger exemplifies.

For countless centuries, India was blanketed with forests and grassland over which the tiger reigned, and human beings did their best to keep out of its way.

The tiger's infrequent intrusion on their lives—its seizure of a prized bullock or, far more rarely, its attack on a human being—was seen as one more inexplicable action of the whimsical gods. "Forest communities accepted the tiger's right to intervene in

*Opposite:* A tiger peers from a leafy hiding place at Bandhavgarh National Park in Madhya Pradesh.

Tiger clawing a tree at Ranthambhore, part of a whole repertoire of marking techniques meant to ensure that no other tigers intrude upon his territory.

their lives," as the tiger expert Valmik Thapar has written; "—that which gave life also had the right to take it away."

This belief helps explain the villagers' apparent nonchalance about living in close proximity with tigers that proved so mystifying to the British. "It would indeed almost appear that the power given to Adam over the beasts of the fields was reversed in India," wrote one District Magistrate. "In an old Hindustani book which I have read, a woman alluding to her death, says she hopes to get along, somehow, until a tiger catches her, as though being killed by a tiger was the ordinary cause of death."

Touring northern India in the spring of 1818, the Marquis of Hastings was equally puzzled when he was shown an island in the Gogra River near Bharatpur on which five tigers were said to live within full view of farmers placidly tending their crops. "It is curious to observe the force of habit," he wrote afterwards.

> Were a tiger to get away from a showman in England, and to be supposed hidden in some of the copses, no person would venture to labour in any of the neighbouring fields. Here, the people not only work close to the usual lair of tigers often seen by them, but actually follow their cattle into these jungles. Nor does this proceed from any expectation that the tiger, if unprovoked, is not likely to attack them; for they have constant instances of the animals' seeking to prey upon men. The danger is one to which their minds have been accustomed from youth, and they consider it a condition inseparable from their existence.

The tiger, though often unseen, was also omnipresent and all-powerful, and there has always existed a wary and understandable ambivalence about it among the people of the forest, a complicated mix of dread and reverence. In some areas, villagers refuse to say the tiger's name for fear of offending it, and among the members

Maharao Umed Singh of Kotah (firing, at upper left) and guests enjoy a day of princely carnage in the royal hunting preserve at Kotah in this miniature painted in 1781. Among the animals milling past his party's weapons: six tigers, a sloth bear, nilghai, and a surprisingly placid stag meant to represent either a chital or a sambar.

of at least one forest tribe, the families of tiger victims were ostracized for having angered the forest deity. Some farmers traditionally offered thanks to tigers for preying upon the deer that otherwise would have ravaged their crops. Others asked their permission before daring to enter the forest. (Hindu and Muslim honey-gatherers alike pray to the same tiger divinity before venturing into the Sunderbans thickets on India's eastern border, where man-eating persists.) Still others did their best to kill tigers with traps and pits and poisoned arrows.

Everything about the tiger embodied magical power. In Rajasthan, burning a bit of its dried flesh ensured that a herdsman's cattle would give birth to healthy calves. Devouring the heart imparted bravery and cunning. A tiger-claw necklace lent courage to anyone who wore it. Tiger whiskers, chopped fine and swallowed with water, warded off danger and guaranteed sexual potency. ("The natives *will* take them," a nineteenth-century British hunter complained. "A tiger skin with its whiskers preserved is a rarity; you cannot keep them. The domestic, who would preserve any other valuable as a most sacred trust, will fail under this temptation.")

The Moghuls, the Muslim invaders who began their conquest of India during the sixteenth century, brought along with them to the subcontinent the notion of hunting for sport—and always on the grandest possible scale. It was the emperor Akbar's custom when on *shikar*, for example, to bring whole armies into the field with him (indeed, his military campaigns were sometimes disguised as sport to fool his enemies). Fifty thousand soldiers are said to have acted as his beaters. They formed a great circle in the jungle fifty miles across, then slowly drew the noose tighter over several days until thousands of terrified beasts—from hares to tigers—were trapped, milling helplessly inside a four-mile ring of wattle screens. Then Akbar rode into this enormous pen and slaughtered everything that moved. When he was sated, which sometimes took five days, first his nobles and then the common soldiers were let in to mop up. During the sanguinary reign of Akbar's son and successor, Jehangir, the

*Left:* Umed Singh shoots again at Kotah, this time sitting up over a buffalo by moonlight. One tiger is already dead or dying; the second, evidently deaf to gunfire, continues to maul the bait.

*Below:* The Emperor Akbar kills a tiger from horseback in this miniature from the *Akbar-Nama*, displaying courage so great, his fawning court biographer wrote, that when "the spectators beheld this the hair on their bodies stood erect and sweat distilled from their pores." Those dazzled spectators presumably did not include the shikaris shown here, who were far too busy trying to dispatch the vanquished tiger's cubs to take much notice.

emperor boasted that he had personally accounted for fourteen thousand animals and seventeen thousand birds.

The style set by the Moghuls was later mimicked by many of the Hindu princes who were otherwise their most implacable opponents, and the enthusiasm some of them showed for unbridled killing survived well into the twentieth century. In 1909, for example, the Maharaja of Rewa laid on a lavish, old-fashioned outing for the otherwise modern-minded Gaekwar Sayaji Rao II of Baroda and his queen. After five days of *shikar*, during which the three rulers managed to account for fifteen tigers, they still hadn't quite had enough. An English clergyman, the Reverend Edward St. Clair Weeden, tutor to the heir to Baroda's throne and a great admirer of his pupil's parents, wrote up what happened next for his mother back home:

> On the way back to Rewa a stop was made at the famous game preserve, a tract of land several square miles in extent enclosed by a high wall, over which not even a tiger could escape. There are three entrances with large gates over which rooms had been built for sportsmen.
>
> For a week, food in large quantities had been placed in this preserve, and then the gates were closed the day before our arrival. As soon as their Highnesses had taken their places in the rooms, the beat began from the end of the preserve farthest from the gates. Presently, the devoted victims began to appear, at first in twos and threes, and then in large herds. There were hundreds of sambar, but when several dozen had fallen, the shooting ceased at the Maharani's request, as she said it was becoming mere butchery. Just then a tigress came along with her cubs: the Maharani had laid aside her rifle, but she caught it up again, and shot one of the cubs. Instantly, the tigress turned

and went down the line of beaters striking at them as she went. Five of them were badly mauled and of these, three died of their wounds afterwards. Her Highness was much concerned at this sad termination of the expedition, which she had so much enjoyed: she requested that she might be kept informed of the condition of the sufferers, and sent suitable compensation to their families.

No one knows how many tigers there were in India when the British began arriving in the seventeenth century—no one knows how many there are now, for that matter—and to get any sense at all of what India's jungles were like before their degradation began, it's necessary to beat one's way through the blood-stained memoirs of British hunters.

If the damage tigers were officially charged with doing is any index, there must have been a very great many of them. "At one time in parts of India at the beginning of the last century," wrote the zoologist and forester Dunbar Brander, in 1923, "tigers were so numerous it seemed to be a question as to whether man or the tiger would survive." In 1796, around the single town of Bhiwapur, tigers were reported to have taken some four hundred lives and finally forced its inhabitants to flee; tigers were routinely seen in broad daylight on the outskirts of Calcutta; and a ring of fires had to be kept burning all night so that they would not stalk their prey through the narrow lanes of Gorakhpur on the border with Nepal.

"It is wonderful to see the number of villages (or rather the sites where they once stood) in Ramghur wholly uncultivated and deserted," wrote the author of *Indian Field Sports* in 1827. "Whenever a tiger carries off a man near a public road or footpath, a stick with a coloured cloth, or a small white triangular flag on a bamboo staff ten or twelve feet high, is erected as a warning to travellers; and every passer-by throws a stone on to the heap, which soon become large heaps in abundance." (During the 1820s, similar cairns were said to have been visible every quarter of a mile or so along the more jungly roads of Mysore, but, as often happened during the Raj, the British misunderstood their meaning; passers-by placed stones on the heap not to commemorate the fallen or warn their fellow travelers, but as holy offerings, to quiet the victim's ghost and persuade the tiger deity to spare their lives.)

In 1822, in the jungles of Kandesh alone, some 500 human beings and 20,000 cattle were said to have fallen prey to animals—mostly tigers. Between 1860 and 1866 in Lower Bengal, tigers took 4,218 lives, and in Kandesh District alone during the 1890s they were still taking an average of 350 lives each year—and another 250 in nearby Jabalpur.

Relative statistics provided some comfort, but not much. "When it is borne in mind that the population of India, including the Native States, is nearly 250,000,000," Dr. J. Fayrer, an officer in the Bengal Medical Service, assured English readers in 1875,

the proportion of deaths is not so large as it at first sight seems to be, and probably would not contrast so very unfavourably with mortality from what should be preventible causes at home—railway accidents, for example! Far be it from me to suggest ought that might appear to involve danger to human life, but I must say that I should regret the complete extinction of tigers with a regret something akin to that with which annihilation of the fox would be regarded in England....

I certainly would not preserve tigers and would encourage their destruction, but by hunting, rather than by poison or the snare. Of course, when no sportsmen are at hand, they should be destroyed without law, when and where they are to be found.

In British India, sportsmen were nearly always at hand. The men who ruled India were young and single, for the most part, easily bored with administrative duties or cantonment life, eager for adventure. "Never was there such a paradise for the hunter," Major General William Rice remembered, "... the whole country then being like an undiscovered land, for on the best district maps was written for miles around, 'No information forthcoming on this part.'"

There were soon few parts of India to which eager British *shikaris* had not gone, and few living things were off-limits to their guns. "We ... blazed away at everything that got up," recalled one unrepentant member of a party of three after a morning's excursion on elephant-back in the terai.

> Before we got back to camp, our pad was like a poulterer's shop. Besides
> the [sarus crane], we shot a florican, a Brahminy duck, a wild goose, a brace
> of *lalseer* or red-tufted mallard, several pintails, grey duck and teal ... also ...
> two or three sandpipers, goggle-eyed plover, two beef-steak birds, or black
> ibis, and a couple of curlew. Pat knocked over a brace of snipe near one of
> the tanks, while I bagged a blue fowl, two grey partridges, a brace of hares
> and two green pigeons, which we got in a small mango grove near a ruined
> village.

But it was the tiger upon which every clerk and subaltern set his heart. "A tiger, seen for the first time at large in its own jungles," wrote one veteran hunter, "is a sight few sportsmen can look on without experiencing a feeling of intense excitement, coupled with an almost uncontrollable desire to possess its head and skin."

The slaughterous thirty-year career of Sir Edward Braddon demonstrates the kind of toll just one zealous hunter could take. Braddon was characteristic of a certain kind of British official, drawn to the Indian jungles but repelled by the people who lived in and around them. He began his griffinage—his Indian apprenticeship—as a clerk in a relative's mercantile house at Calcutta, but spent every weekend banging away at snipe on Howrah and Kanchrapur *jheels* (ponds)—fifty-one pair at Kanchrapur without a miss one especially sharp-eyed morning, and forty-nine more the next—and he alternated bird shooting with pig-sticking in the dense fields of grain that once stood where international jets now land at Dum-Dum airport.

On one twelve-day hunt, organized by the collector of Moorshedabad, and employing nearly one hundred elephants to beat through the tall *kassia* grass, he and six other horsemen managed to spear ninety-nine wild boar.

After his time in Calcutta, Braddon ran indigo plantations in what is now Bihar, then moved to Deogarh, the site of a celebrated Shiva temple and of Hindu pilgrimages since the time of the *Puranas*, surrounded by jungles, where he served as "magistrate, collector, judge &c." He was elaborately scornful of the Indians in his charge.

> There was a standing difficulty about the chief *panda*ship [priesthood] that was
> always at hand to occupy my diplomatic skill—a difficulty that arose, if I rightly
> remember, out of this *de facto* high priest having failed to observe the rule of
> celibacy required by his office. He was a man of strong family instincts, and

would not give up his wife and children; he was also a man of marked acquisitiveness, and would not forgo the emolumens of the chief pandaship—and no diplomacy of mine could adjust this difficulty. When I left Deogarh, after nearly five years, that obstinate flamen was still battling with a less domestic priest who sought to oust him.... Then the other 359 pandas were always at loggerheads with each other or with any available outsider—frequently about their *chelas,* or disciples, but about anything or anybody when the *chela* failed as motive for a row. And, finally, the wretched pilgrims gave constant trouble, in that they were plundered by the priests and other robbers no less professional, who found their opportunity of thieving in the crowded town, just as if Deogarh had been Trafalgar Square on a demonstration day.

Braddon listened to such disputes for ten to twelve hours a day, he recalled, "with one reservation—that whenever news was brought of a tiger, panther or bear anywhere within twenty miles, my court was to be closed *instanter.*"

His predecessor had not hunted, according to Braddon, and predators had therefore multipled and were "generally, if not universally, man-eaters.... Young and old alike, their prey was, on occasion, man or woman: they killed the wretched woodcutters, or the old women who picked up sticks in the jungle; they carried off the wayfarer from the highroad; they broke into the grass huts of the sleeping peasant and carried off the husband from his wife's side...." (Some sort of epidemic may have reduced the predators' natural prey, forcing them first to look to domestic animals for their sustenance and then to the men and women who owned them.)

In any case, there were four tigers close at hand, roaming the jungle on the edge of town, "whose confirmed habit it was to devour Deoghurites." They routinely hauled victims from their huts after dark and "even stalked abroad by day, as I saw for myself very shortly after my arrival, when one of them sauntered through my compound some time before sunset, as if bent on making an afternoon call on the new *Hakim* [magistrate]."

The priests warned Braddon that nothing could be done: Shiva himself protected the tigers. "It only struck me as ridiculous that they should talk in this way to one who thirsted for the blood of many tigers": he recalled, "a score of [Shivas], backed up by ten thousand *pandas,* could not have quenched my tigercidal thirst, or stayed me in the attempt to slake it."

Braddon shot three of the man-eaters within half a mile of his bungalow, the first from a *machan* (a platform constructed in a tree), the next two from the back of a borrowed elephant. An Indian hunter killed the fourth with a spring-bow. Braddon tied each of the tigers to the pad of his elephant and marched it through the main bazaar so that crowds could come out to see it and shout: "*Waugh! Waugh!* (Well done! Well done!)" Even the *pandas* left the ghats to cheer:

Wonderful are the Hindoos for accepting the inevitable! Tell one of these that he must take castor-oil, and he will drain the oleaginous cup to the dregs and smack his lips. Tell him that his leg must be amputated, and he will present the limb for dismemberment, and smile as he sees it severed. Tell him that he is to be hanged, and, with no touch of emotion whatever, he will reply *"Ji hookm"* ("Whatever is ordered"), just as if he had been told that he must have his corns cut. Our tiger was the inevitable to these *pandas....*

*Pages 38–39:* In a jungle made unusually luxuriant by monsoon rains, a fourteen-month-old male cub explores a crumbling fortress wall at Ranthambhore.

Three lithographs from *Tiger-Shooting in India*, published in 1857 by Lieutenant William Rice of the 25th Bombay Native Infantry. In the first, a wounded tigress seizes the lieutenant's shooting companion. The shikaris, Rice wrote, "with admirable coolness," continued to pass him loaded weapons until four more shots finally brought her down. The terrified hunter somehow survived his mauling. At center, shikaris belonging to the Bhil tribe rejoice at the less eventful death of another tigress. Below, back in camp, Rice flays one tiger; the pelt of another has already been pegged out to dry; and in the distance, a third tiger is being brought in to be skinned.

Because he had no elephants of his own, Braddon was often forced to shoot his tigers from a platform, but he thought it unsporting: "I always had the feeling that in shooting tigers from a *machan* I was an unworthy foe—a mere assassin—and, at the best, that the performance, however largely beneficent, was distinctly inglorious. The peasants whose cows or wives or sons were killed by tigers were other-minded.... They saw no merit, no good point whatever in a tiger, which I, rightly or wrongly, regarded as the veritable king of beasts...."

Shooting from the ground, he believed, offered the best sport of all, and it had provided him with his most memorable day in the field,

> the proudest moment of my life ... when I bagged a brace right and left.
> They came out of the jungle close together—a tiger and his consort; and I had hardly realized that this king of beasts had walked into the open, when the queen was there, two or three yards behind her sovereign lord. Slowly, they came forth, with backward glance, that told of some bewilderment, and on the female's part, it may be conceived, some curiosity. No fear quickened the pulse or stride of the twain; no suspicion of my presence crossed their minds. Calmly those splendid beauties of the forest sauntered on, giving me full broadside shots at a distance of some twenty-five yards. Crack! crack! right and left the bullets from my smooth-bore went home, and the two tigers dropped—the female never to rise again. The tiger, terribly hard hit, rose and made a feeble demonstration in my direction, but another shot settled it; and there were the couple bagged, and the curtain dropped upon this splendid drama of the forest.

"What number of animals I killed during my four and a half years at Deogharh," Braddon continued, "I cannot say.... At first, I saved the skins as trophies, and had a fairly large bungalow carpeted with them from end to end; but they smelt objectionably in the rains, and tripped me up in the hot weather and I got rid of them. Then I kept skulls ranged upon shelves until I made my house a Golgotha, and was driven to cast those oseous relics forth; and when I left Deogarh ... I took with me no memento whatever of those four and a half years' shikar...."

Braddon did not confine his shooting to official duties. For thirteen years, he spent his off-time with four or five friends on organized tiger shoots in the *terai*, and in his 1872 memoir called *Life in India: A Series of Sketches Showing Something of the Anglo Indian—the Land He Lives In—And the People Among Whom He Lives*, he recalled just some of what was required in the way of logistics.

To begin with, elephants had to be borrowed from local Rajahs and *zemindars* (great landowners). Then, cartloads of food and drink had to be brought in before the hunters arrived. Each hunter came with his own train of domestic servants. Each elephant demanded two *mahouts* to care for and drive it; there was a man for every two camels, one or two men to every cart.

Then, there were the *khalassies* (tent-pitchers), *moochees* (skinners), *shikarees* (who gathered news of tigers), *dak-wallahs* (who ran relays to and from the nearest railhead, sometimes 150 miles away, carrying mail and newspapers), half a dozen agents to supply suitable food for the mixture of Hindus and Muslims in camp; and, should one of the hunters happen to be a government official, there was also sure to be an encampment of *amlahs* (clerks and petty officials) and their dependents.

This great assemblage came together at the height of the Indian summer:

... [T]he month is April or May and the "merry, merry sunshine" is better calculated to make the head dizzy than the heart gay, but the sportsman ignores the thermometer altogether and enjoys himself as thoroughly as though the temperature were 60 degrees lower than it is. Rising at any hour between 5 a.m. and 8 a.m., he takes his breakfast in the mess tent and prepares for the day's campaign. At noon the tiger comes down from the forest to spend the heat of the day in swamps or open patches of cool green grass, and as it is in his daily haunts that he is to be sought, the hunt does not begin before twelve.... Then the howdah elephants are brought round to the tents, and the howdahs are fitted with the batteries of rifles and smooth bores, ammunition, bottles of cold tea or something stronger, cheroot boxes and other necessaries, that include sometimes an umbrella and a blanket (the blanket being taken to throw over the head should an incautious elephant break up a hive of wild bees and send the angry swarm round the heads of its riders). And then the sportsmen mount and are jogged off upon an expedition that will be terminated some time after dark. Once afield, the party submits to very strict discipline, and one leader directs the movements of the band.

When a tiger is supposed to be near at hand this commander will signal that there is to be no general firing, and while that order remains unrevoked, deer of many kinds (*sambhur, bara-singha,* fallow-deer, and hog-deer), wild pigs, peafowl, florican, black partridge, &c., crash away in the grass below,

In an engraving by Thomas Landseer, based on a drawing by O. P. Trench, two British hunters who threw a firecracker into a likely thicket get more than they bargained for — two angry tigers at once.

or rise in the air above, without having their flight quickened or arrested by a shot. When general firing is permitted, there is often a constant fusillade, closely resembling rifles on parade, and every now and then some feathered or four-footed quarry is picked up and padded on one of the elephants of the line. But the real excitement commences when (in solemn silence, as far as men are concerned), the line of elephants forces its way through the long, dense grass that is supposed to hold a tiger. If it be in a swamp, there is the additional excitement engendered by the possibility of one's elephants sinking in it and staying there; and as at each step the bulky animal goes deep into the treacherous bog—now swaying low on one side, then on the other—it becomes a matter of anxious consideration whether it will ever get its feet out to advance another step or return. Shaken from side to side of his howdah, and often with his view intercepted by the grass and reeds rising above his head, the tiger-shooter stands in his howdah, rifle in hand, prepared for that moment when he may catch a glimpse of a yellow skin with black bars upon it. He hears animals breaking through the jungle close at hand, but though he cannot see them he knows from the style of their going that they are not what he looks for.

At last the tiger is sighted (perhaps two or more are sighted at the same time), and there are shouts of "bagh, bagh" (tiger, tiger), from the natives, and shots from every sportsman who has seen, or thinks he has seen it. Then there are cries of "lugga, lugga" (hit, hit), from the natives, who always say that an animal is hit however little reason there may be for forming such a conclusion; and possibly a general scrimmage in which the tiger is apparently omnipresent—now on the head of one elephant, then on the tail of another—until he lies hors de combat on the grass and snarls his life away.

When the tiger is being padded (i.e. lashed upon the pad of an elephant that does not carry a howdah), the Anglo-Indians refresh themselves, and the contents of the tiffin basket (carried on a pad elephant devoted to this purpose) are discussed, while an animated argument may ensue as to the mode by which the tiger came to his death. As the skin of the animal is the especial trophy of him whose bullet was the first to hit it, each sportsman brings himself to believe that his was the lucky shot, and boldly asserts what he believes. "I hit him with my first barrel just above the shoulder, and my second touched him in his hind leg," "I know I hit him because I saw him swerve as I fired," and similar remarks are current; and the interior of the tiger must be a rich lead mine if it contains all the bullets that are said to have passed into it. But subsequent investigation, when the tiger is skinned close to the camp, proves that some four instead of forty bullets have [hit the animal], and inquiry conducted upon judicial principles and with all regard to laws of evidence, frequently clears up the point as to the rightful claimant of the first effective missile.

The hunters' missiles were very often effective. Braddon noted that a party of five that included Sir George Udney Yule, conqueror of the Santhal tribesmen and slayer of well over four hundred tigers; Herky Ross, then the champion rifle-shot of India, and Bob Aitken, a much-decorated hero of the Indian mutiny, shot forty tigers in a single trip to the terai—"a record," Braddon noted, "that has never been touched, I fancy, before or since, not even when tigers have been netted and imprisoned and put down for the shooters." (In fact, the king of Nepal would break that record all on his own in 1939, slaying forty-one in one hunt in his private reserve just over the border.)

James Inglis, a rough contemporary of Sir Edward Braddon's, recalled a still more effective method of hunting from elephant-back—setting the whole terai landscape on fire:

> In the howdah we carry ample supplies of vesuvians [fireworks]. We light and drop these as they blaze into the dried grass and withered leaves as we move along, and soon a mighty wall of roaring flame behind us, attests the presence of the destroying element. We go diagonally upwind, and the flames and smoke thus surge and roar and curl and roll, in dense blinding volumes to the rear and leeward of our line. The roaring of the flames sounds like a maddened surf of an angry sea, dashing in thunder against an iron-bound coast. The leaping flames mount up in fiery columns, illuminating the fleecy clouds of smoke with an unearthly glare. The noise is deafening; at times some of the elephants get quite nervous at the fierce roar of the flames behind, and try to bolt across the country. The fire serves two good purposes. It burns up the old withered grass, making room for the fresh succulent sprouts, and it keeps all the game in front of the line, driving the animals before us, as they are afraid to break back and face the roaring wall of flame. A seething, surging sea of flame, several miles long, encircling the whole country in its fiery belt, sweeping along at night with the roar of a storm-tossed sea; the flames flickering, swelling and leaping up in the dark night, the fiery particles rushing along amid clouds of lurid smoke, and the glare of the serpent-like line reddening the horizon, is one of those magnificent spectacles that can only be witnessed at rare intervals among the experiences of a sojourn in India. Words fail to depict its grandeur, and the utmost skill of [Gustave] Doré could not render on canvas, the weird, unearthly magnificence of a jungle fire....
>
> [The elephants move together] like a wall. You stand erect in the howdah, your favorite gun at the ready; your attendant beside you is as excited as yourself, and sways from side to side to peer into the gloomy depths of the jungle; in front, the mahout wriggles on his seat, as if by his motion he could urge the elephant to a quicker advance. He digs his toes savagely into his elephant behind the ear; the line is closing up; every eye is fixed on the moving jungle ahead. The roaring of the flames behind and the crushing of the ... reeds as the elephants force their ponderous frames through the intertwisted stems and foliage, are the only sounds that greet the ear. Suddenly you see the tawny yellow hide, as the tiger slouches along. Your gun rings out a reverberating challenge, as your fatal bullet speeds on its errand. To right and left the echoes ring, as shot after shot is fired at the bounding robber. Then the line closes up, and you form a circle round the stricken beast, and watch his mighty limbs quiver in the death agony, and as he falls over dead and powerless for future harm, you raise the heartfelt, pulse-stirring cheer, that finds an echo in every brother sportsman's heart.

The pulses of Inglis and his brother sportsmen raced especially fast when they wounded but did not immediately kill their quarry:

A tiger wounded in the spine ... is the most exciting spectacle. Paralyzed in the limbs, he wheels around, roaring and biting at everything within his reach. In 1874, I shot one in the spine, and watched his furious movements for some time before I put him out of his misery. I threw him a pad from one of the elephants, and the way he tore ... it gave me some faint idea of his fury and ferocity. He looked the very personification of impotent viciousness; the incarnation of devilish rage.

Very occasionally a tiger got the opportunity to wreak a kind of revenge. Inglis tells of one Mr. Aubert, "a Benares planter," one of several hunters who first "spined" a tiger, then "gathered round the prostrate monster to watch its death struggle." The sound and fury evidently "demoralized" Aubert's elephant, which bolted, heading for a tree with low-hanging branches that would have splintered his howdah. "To save himself, Aubert made a leap for the branch, the elephant forging madly ahead; and the howdah being smashed like match-wood, fell on the tiger below, who was tearing and clawing at everything within his reach. Poor Aubert got hold of the branch with his hands," and hung on, dangling over the tiger, which was still "mad with agony and fury ... a picture of demoniac rage." Finally, the "poor fellow could hold no longer and fell right on the tiger. It was nearly at its last gasp, but it caught hold of Aubert by the foot, and in the final paroxysm of pain and rage chawed the foot clean off, and the poor fellow died the next day from the shock and loss of blood."

Three officers of the 93rd Highlanders return from a fortnight's hunt in the Deccan. Their bag includes five tigers, a leopard, black buck, chital, and sambar. Somehow, the tethered fawn and two tiger cubs survived intact.

British blood was rarely lost. When things went badly, it was almost always the local villagers recruited to drive the animals in front of British guns who were made to suffer. Sometimes it was at the hands of the sahibs who had hired them, disappointed when a promised tiger failed to pass beneath their *machan:* "Under such circumstances," wrote Colonel Julius Barras in 1885, "I have known an ordinarily just and kind gentleman to turn upon the natives and beat them. This should never be done, as it prevents them from bringing in news [of tigers] on future occasions."

More often, the villagers had to fear the animals themselves, and Colonel Barras urged would-be hunters not to overlook that possibility when budgeting for their hunts: "[Some] expenses ... can, of course, be reckoned upon before starting, but there are others of a less certain nature. Occasionally, beaters are killed, and then the compensation paid to their families is often heavy. Or an elephant may be sacrificed, and then you would be expected to pay for him! But these are dismal considerations, and apt, perhaps, to damp the rising ardour!"

Rare accidents aside, in the struggle between the hunter and the hunted, the hunted hadn't a chance. "The influx of Englishmen ... lessened the ravages of wild beasts," wrote the civil servant and naturalist Edward Lockwood, "and besides the legitimate hunting which goes on when there is any chance of sport, the Government offers so high a reward for the destruction of tigers and leopards that a hundred skins have been brought to me by one party of hunters ... using set bows and poisoned arrows."

Davies Digby Davies, an officer of the Bombay Police and commander of a special unit charged with keeping down the number of tigers in Kandesh, killed better than two hundred and fifty of them all by himself, not counting another fifty or so shot on leave. "My biggest bag for one year...," he recalled, "was thirty-one and for one week, six. At one time, indeed, I remember being almost tired of shooting tigers, they were so plentiful, and in so many cases shot without any greater effort on my part than holding the rifle straight."

According to one writer, some 20,000 to 30,000 tigers were killed in India between 1860 and 1960; according to another, more than 100,000 tigers were shot between 1800 and 1900. Still, the naturalist E. P. Gee estimated that there were some forty thousand tigers left in India at the century's turn, and 40 percent of the subcontinent is then thought still to have been covered by forest.

CHAPTER THREE
# THE LARGE-HEARTED GENTLEMAN

It was just before lunch on April 20, 1955, and my father was seated on the living-room sofa in our New Delhi house, enjoying a beer and finishing the newspaper.

The front-page story that morning was the death of Jim Corbett in Kenya the previous day, and it was accompanied by a familiar photograph of the great hunter in his old age, peering fondly at a small bird perched on his index finger.

Siri Ram, the bearer, announced that lunch was ready, bent to gather up my father's glass, then froze, staring at the newspaper.

"My old sahib," he said excitedly, pointing to the newspaper. "Why he's there?"

"I'm afraid he died," my father said, putting down the paper.

I had already established that Siri Ram came from the Kumaon Hills where Corbett had once lived, and he had once or twice made it clear that the souvenirs of slaughter that I brought home from the field were not up to the standards set by someone for whom he had worked long before; but I had no idea that he had ever actually known my hero.

"I was a boy when I worked for him," he said, his eyes filled with tears. "He was a good man. No sahibs like that these days." He fled to the kitchen.

That judgment was a little hard on my father, who was doing his best to be the sort of sahib of whom Siri Ram might be expected to approve.

But he was right about Jim Corbett.

The tiger," Corbett wrote in *Man-Eaters of Kumaon*, his first and best-loved book, "is a large-hearted gentleman with boundless courage." Such courtly anthropomorphism is understandably out of fashion these days, but the same description could justly be applied to the man who wrote it. For Corbett represented within himself—as hunter and conservationist, author and outdoorsman, and loyal subject of the Crown—all the gentlemanly attributes of the British imperial system at its best. The tragedy was that partly because he also shared that system's worst delusions, he became its victim, ending his days in sad, self-imposed exile from the land he never stopped loving.

Edward James Corbett, of mixed Irish and Manx ancestry, was born in India and therefore considered "Domiciled"—the scornful epithet was "country-bottled"—relegated to the lowest rank among India's white rulers, whose caste system was only slightly more yielding than that of those they ruled. Domiciled Britons were thought better than coolies by upper-class Britons—they were welcome, for example, on the Upper Mall in the Himalayan hill station of Naini Tal, where Corbett was born in 1875, from which Indians and beasts of burden were once expressly barred unless they were carrying out some errand for their British masters—and they were thought more desirable than persons of mixed British and Indian ancestry. But they could never expect to serve in prestigious administrative posts or to climb very high in the Army or to marry any of the flock of English girls who came out to India each winter in search of husbands, even though without them and their forebears there would have been no British Raj at all.

Corbett's own father, Christoper Corbett, the Naini Tal postmaster, had helped lift the siege of Delhi during the 1857 Mutiny. That sudden and bloody rebellion by Indian troops thought faithful to the British Queen had traumatized the Raj. Afterwards, the British never fully trusted their Indian subjects. Corbett and his brothers and sisters were steeped in Mutiny lore: their father's younger brother had been tied to a stake and burned alive by the rebels; their mother's first husband had been pulled from his horse and hacked to death. No matter how gentle and amiable Indians seemed, the children were taught, one had always to be on guard.

Christopher Corbett died suddenly when James was four, leaving his wife with a summer home above Naini Tal, a winter home fifteen miles down the mountain road at Kaladhungi, and a turbulent brood of twelve children to raise and educate on a widow's meager pension. The Corbetts were poor but proud. Appearances were kept up; stoicism and self-sacrifice encouraged. His mother, Corbett recalled, "though she had the courage of Joan of Arc and Nurse Clavell combined, was as gentle and timid as a dove."

He remembered his boyhood as a sort of forest idyll. Lying in bed at Kaladhungi, he listened night after night to the cries of the animals that filled the dark surrounding forests, learning first to understand and eventually to mimic nearly all of them. (As a grown man, he could call a serpent eagle down out of the sky using a split reed to imitate the piercing call of a fawn in distress, and he once impersonated a leopard so persuasively that a British hunter and a leopard crept toward him simultaneously.) In the early mornings the small boy eagerly paced the sandy bed of the Baur River that ran near the house, studying fresh tracks to discover what had happened there the night before. Corbett's uncanny understanding of the plants and animals and birds of the Kumaon Hills had virtually been bred into him.

Corbett's earliest hunting was done to fill the family larder. He had to account for every shell. "Good shooting," an old friend wrote, "was to him an obligation rather than an accomplishment." But his increasingly frequent trips into the forest may have had another meaning, too. The Corbett household must have been a tumultuous place: years later, Corbett would confess that as adults, neither he nor his older sister Maggie ever felt "happy in a crowd." By the age of nine, Corbett was spending several days at a time in the forest. An aged family gardener sometimes accompanied him, but he slept in the open, and his only real protection was an ancient muzzle-loading shotgun whose one good barrel was lashed to the stock with brass wire.

He attended school at Naini Tal, finding time between classes to shoot and prepare the skins of some 480 species of hill birds for a cousin who was preparing a field guide. Then, at seventeen, he signed on with the Indian railways, one of the few organizations hospitable to young Domiciled Englishmen. He was a fuel inspector at first, supervising the felling of timber, and then he became a transshipment inspector at Mokameh Ghat, a dusty outstation on the bank of the Ganges east of Benares. There was nothing remotely glamorous about this job, which each year for just over two decades consisted of seeing to it that a million tons of goods were ferried across the river from one rail line to another. But he did gain an extraordinary reputation for industry and fairness among the Indian laborers who worked for him, eating nothing but lentils and unleavened bread when times were lean, just as they

Jim Corbett and the immense male he called the Bachelor of Powalgarh and hunted down in 1930.

did, and distributing 80 percent of his own annual profits among the men at Christmas.

Nor was there anything especially adventurous about his daily life after he left the railway at thirty-nine, without ever having moved up in its hierarchy. He moved back to Naini Tal, went into the hardware and real estate business, and did about as well as a country-born Englishman could expect. He served on the town council and presented the town with a brightly painted band shell. But he was not, until late in life, asked to join the Naini Tal Yacht Club, and even after he did join, a friend recalled, he rarely went there, being unused to "the elevated society." (To be fair, admission to the club was never easily achieved: the club president, Sir William Stampe, was once said to have blackballed the wealthy head of a gentleman's outfitters' firm by saying: "If I wish to see my tailor, I shall go to his shop.")

Winters were spent at Kaladhungi, in a small bungalow at the edge of a village called Choti Haldwani, of which he and his sister Maggie became the benevolent proprietors. Corbett adjudicated family disputes among his tenants, calmed tension between Hindus and Muslims, provided imported seed; he even acted as unofficial physician, dispensing pills and unguents to sick or injured villagers. And he acted as their protector, building a nine-kilometer stone wall around the village and its fields to keep deer and wild boar out of their crops and eliminating any predators that menaced their cattle and buffalo.

His India was always that of the peasant. "Simple, honest, brave, loyal, hard-working souls," he called them once, "whose daily prayer to God, and to whatever Government is in power, is to give them security of life and of property to enable them to enjoy the fruits of their labors." Modern India—urban, educated, increasingly stirred by politics, increasingly impatient with British rule—was alien to him, and always menacing.

There were thousands of other Britons scattered in small places all across India in those days, living similarly quiet lives, largely unknown beyond the villages over which they held sway. It was Corbett's shooting skill and encyclopedic knowledge of the jungle that set him apart. As early as 1906, requests began to reach him begging that he come up into the hills to track down a tiger or leopard that had begun to prey on man. Sometimes the afflicted villagers themselves petitioned him, their genuine terror evident beneath the inflated language of the scribes whose pens they hired:

Respected Sir,
We the public are in great distress. By the fear of the tiger we cannot watch our wheat crop so the deers have nearly ruined it. We cannot go into the forest for the fodder grass nor can we enter our cattles into the forest to graze. . . . We have heard that your kind self have killed many man-eating tigers and leopards. So we the public venture to suggest that you very kindly take trouble to come to this place and shoot this tiger and save the public from this calamity. For this act of kindness the public will be highly obliged and will pray for your long life and prosperity.

More often, local British officials did the asking, having exhausted every other remedy. But it took considerable evidence to coax Corbett into the field. He believed that any animal which had struck once or twice under special circumstances—while guarding cubs, for example, or when disturbed on a kill—should be given the benefit of the doubt. It was only habitual man-eaters that interested him, and even when there was no question that an animal was guilty, he never volunteered to shoot it: as a Domiciled Englishman he would not go where he was not wanted. And he always set two conditions: All offers of a reward had to be withdrawn before he arrived, and all other hunters had to leave the forest. His reasons were at once principled and practical. "I am sure all sportsmen share my aversion to being classed as a reward-hunter," he wrote, "and are as anxious as I to avoid being shot."

Corbett consented to hunt down at least a dozen man-eaters between 1906 and 1941. There is no way of estimating how many human lives his efforts saved, but the combined total of men, women, and children those twelve animals are thought to have killed before he stopped them was more than one thousand five hundred. (Corbett's very first man-eater, the Champawat tiger, alone was responsible for 436 deaths.)

He seems never to have been anything but ambivalent about these successful expeditions. Once, after weeks of fruitless stalking of a man-eater in the full blast of the Indian summer, up and down the slopes of the Himalayan foothills, he came upon his quarry lying on its back behind a log, paws in the air, fast asleep. Corbett crept closer, rifle raised, until he was within five feet, then fired two bullets into the animal's brain. The tiger died without moving. It had been steadily killing and eating human beings for years, one every few days. The last—a woman cutting grass in the forest—had been killed less than a week before Corbett found it dozing.

At the sound of the shots, a crowd of villagers hurried to the site to see for themselves that the animal that had terrorized them for so long was truly dead and to cheer the man who had risked his own life to rid them of it. Corbett might have been forgiven had he shared at least a little of their exultation. Instead, he felt depressed.

*Opposite: A nearly full-grown female cub rests in the branch of a tree; adult tigers are generally too big and too heavy to like climbing so high.*

"The finish," he wrote later, "had not been satisfactory, for I had killed the animal . . . in his sleep." He continued:

My personal feelings in the matter are I know of little interest to others, but it occurs to me that possibly you [the reader] also may think it was not cricket, and in that case I should like to put some arguments before you that I used on myself, in the hope that you will find them more satisfactory than I did. These arguments were (a) the tiger was a man-eater that was better dead than alive, (b) therefore it made no difference whether he was awake or asleep when killed, and (c) that had I walked away when I saw his belly moving up and down [indicating that he was sleeping] I should have been morally responsible for the deaths of all the human beings he killed thereafter. All good and sound arguments, you will admit, for having acted as I did; but the regret remains that through fear of consequences to myself or for fear of losing the only chance I might ever get, or possibly a combination of the two, I did not awaken the sleeping animal and give him a sporting chance.

The man-eating leopard of Rudraprayag, the most celebrated of all Corbett's quarries and the only one to which he would eventually devote an entire book, officially killed one hundred and fifty people between 1918 and 1926. But because it operated along the twisting mountain trail that leads up to the Hindu shrines of Kedernath and Badrinath, to which some sixty thousand pilgrims made their way on foot each year, its depredations were widely publicized, both in India and abroad. For eight years, no one dared move along that road after dusk; no villager living in the nearby hills stirred from his home.

The leopard was a big male, strong enough to carry its kills up to four miles, if necessary, and it had grown very bold, first taking only victims foolish enough to sleep outdoors, then banging down doors or leaping through windows to get at them, finally methodically clawing its way through the mud or thatch walls of their huts. Rewards were posted. Hundreds of special gun licenses were issued. Amateur sportsmen and local officials sat up for the leopard. Army officers were encouraged to spend their leaves tracking it. Nothing worked. The animal eluded every trap. Poisons seemed only to encourage it. Twenty other leopards were destroyed, but the man-eater remained at large and hungry, and angry questions began to be asked in the British Parliament.

Finally, A. W. Ibbotson, deputy commissioner of the district and an old hunting companion of Corbett's, persuaded him to try his hand. Corbett had been reluctant to intrude at first: "I imagined that people were falling over each other in their eagerness . . . and that in those circumstances a stranger would not be welcome." In any case, he arrived in the early autumn of 1925.

Once Corbett was on the man-eater's trail, however, his tenacity was astonishing. One of the reasons his accounts of his own adventures are so vivid and persuasive is that he never flinched from detailing his own weaknesses and frustration. *The Man-Eating Leopard of Rudraprayag* is a chronicle of terror as well as bravery, of missed opportunities as well as jungle skills, of bad luck as well as persistence. Corbett sat over the corpse of a pregnant woman in the rain most of one night, and in the pitch blackness failed to make out the leopard as it slipped beneath him, its passage marked only by an eerie, inexplicable sound, he said, "like the soft rustle of a woman's silk dress."

A leopard takes the late-afternoon sun; its lying so casually in the open suggests that the far-larger resident tiger with which it must compete for food is far away.

He spent twenty nights alone on the top of a sixty-foot tower overlooking the only bridge across a gorge, tormented by stinging ants and clinging to the tower's flat, featureless top to keep from being blown off by the stiff winds that whipped up the valley. He was rewarded for all his time and trouble by the sight of precisely one animal trotting over the bridge, an oblivious jackal.

Sleeping in a thorn enclosure, he woke to the screams of his cook, who had opened one eye to see the leopard crouched above him in a tree, ready to spring. Before Corbett could get his rifle to his shoulder, the animal bounded away. A few nights later, he was sure he'd caught the man-eater in a leg trap; he fired at the struggling animal in the darkness and succeeded only in snapping the chain that held it there. Corbett tracked it down on foot and killed it—only to find that, although it had earlier stalked a human victim, it was the wrong leopard. After ten weeks of this, Corbett was near collapse from exhaustion. Ibbotson ordered him home to recuperate.

It took him nearly ten months to recover, during which the leopard killed ten more people. He tried to trap it again when he got back the following spring, and once the trap did close on the man-eater's leg, but two of its steel teeth had broken off, allowing the animal just room enough to slip free again. Corbett spent another night in a tree so fiercely lashed by the wind that he had to tie his rifle to the trunk and tear off as many branches as he could reach to cut down wind resistance. Nonetheless, he managed to call up the leopard and lure it toward him; all seemed to be progressing well, until the approaching man-eater encountered a female leopard en route and settled down to an evening of noisy mating just out of rifle range.

Still another night was spent sitting on the ground in a village courtyard only a few yards from the half-eaten body of a small boy. There was no moon, and when Corbett suddenly felt fur rub against his bare knee he was sure that the leopard had found him at last. Instead, it was a small kitten that had been locked out of its hut. He placed it inside his jacket, where it purred and fell asleep. The leopard did approach the village that night but again encountered another leopard, a male this time, setting off a long yowling fight during which the kill was forgotten.

Finally, on the last of eleven nights spent in a big mango tree on the pilgrim road, the man-eater appeared in plain sight. A flashlight was attached to Corbett's rifle. He clicked it on, took aim, and fired. At the shot, the flashlight blinked out. But the leopard at last lay dead.

Characteristically, Corbett's initial emotion was regret. The dead leopard's "only crime, not against the laws of nature but against the laws of man," he wrote, "was that he'd shed human blood with no object of terrorizing man, but only in order that he might live." His friend Ibbotson literally danced with joy at the news. Corbett asked for a pot of tea, took a hot bath, and went to sleep. Later in the day, thousands of people from the surrounding hills converged to see the leopard and offer thanks to their deliverer. Corbett was reluctantly persuaded to receive them, standing tall and silent as, one by one, they filed past to pour rose and marigold petals around his feet.

Like that other solitary British hero, Lawrence of Arabia, Corbett seems always to have been dissatisfied even with his most dramatic triumphs, to have genuinely feared and distrusted the praise his actions won. Like Lawrence, too, he appears to have relished punishing himself. "No greater pleasure can a man know than the cessation of great pain," Corbett once quoted approvingly. He had no bedroom of his own at Kaladhungi for many years, sleeping in a tent beside the house while his sister slept inside. Once on a tiger's trail, he often marched through the hills at a twenty-five-mile-a-day clip, eating nothing for up to sixty-four hours at a stretch. Such strenuous deprivation "had no injurious effect upon me," he wrote, "beyond taking a little flesh off my bones."

In 1929 a heavy rifle went off accidentally beside his left ear, piercing his eardrum, scorching his ear. Nonetheless, when Corbett was asked to hunt down the Tala Des man-eater, a tigress responsible for another one hundred and fifty deaths, he did not hesitate. The pursuit lasted several weeks, during which an abscess steadily grew within his ear, closing his left eye, immobilizing his head and neck, making every step agony. He never even slowed his pace, sitting up night after night though half-blind and almost wholly deaf (his right ear had been damaged earlier), and nearly incoherent with pain and fever. Finally, as he waited for the man-eater in the branches of still another tree, the abscess burst. "Not into my brain as I feared it would," he reported cheerily, "but out through my nose and left ear." He fainted; but he got his tigress.

News of his exploits inevitably reached the newspapers and was passed around the best clubs. The rich and well-born began to seek him out. He was asked to orchestrate elaborate shoots for important people: generals, government officials, maharajas, the Viceroy himself, Lord Linlithgow. These hunts were the antithesis of his own stealthy pursuits. Hundreds of beaters shouted their way through the forests and grasslands, and specially trained elephants delicately retrieved with their trunks the partridges and peafowl the guests and their ladies downed. Corbett professed to be astonished at all the attention he received—"I, a mere man in the street, with no official connection to the Government."

But, in fact, he had become the most famous sportsman in India, and it cannot have been lost on him that when he was in his forest even the most socially exalted amateur had to stand in his shadow. If one witness can be believed, he went to considerable lengths to ensure that he retained his premier position. One year, he and Colonel J. N. Powell, another country-born Kumaon *shikari*, were asked to ready adjacent forest blocks for an upcoming viceregal visit. Powell arrived late, and found that all the young buffalo in the surrounding villages had already been bought up by Corbett. When he asked to be allowed to purchase one or two for bait, his rival turned him down: there was a huge male that regularly traveled through his block, he said, and he wanted to keep it within range until the Viceroy arrived. Because of this apparent breach of sportsmanship, Powell never spoke to Corbett again, and he took an especially sweet revenge: He lured the massive tiger into his territory and shot it himself.

But Corbett's own views were slowly changing. Annual hunting trips to the teeming East African savannah during the 1920s reminded him of what India's forests must have been like before the coming of the British. He was appalled at the ever greater number of hunters, British and Indian, pushing through the forests he had always considered his alone, and dismayed by the policies of the provincial Forest Department, which considered the jungles under its care a source of profit from timber rather than a haven for wildlife.

Eager to pass on his love of the forest to the next generation, Corbett began appearing before groups of schoolchildren in Naini Tal and performing a sort of one-man jungle oratorio, during which he imitated in turn the cries of each bird and animal in the forest as it heralded the tiger's approach. For the finale, he always asked that the lights be turned off in the hall, warned those with faint hearts to leave, then gave the full roar of a tiger, a sound guaranteed to electrify the most blasé schoolboy.

He helped create the Association for the Preservation of Game in the United Provinces of India and the All-India Conference for the Preservation of Wild Life; founded and edited a short-lived natural history magazine, *Indian Wildlife*, dedicated to the proposition that "a bird in the bush is worth two in the hand"; and worked to establish India's first national park in the Kumaon Hills. (Hailey Park, named after an old hunting patron, Sir Malcolm Hailey, governor of the United Provinces, was inaugurated in 1934.)

In 1936, he published an appeal to the people of the United Provinces. He had visited a small village not far from his own, he wrote, where a few seemingly unimportant changes had dangerously altered the ancient balance between man and nature. The village had once been ringed by dense jungle filled with enough hooved animals to keep tigers from menacing the villagers' cattle.

Then, gun licenses had been made more readily available and some villagers found it more profitable to poach deer and sell their meat in the nearby bazaar than to cultivate the land. Simultaneously, lantana, a fast-spreading South American plant, had escaped from some British memsahib's flower pot and spread everywhere, strangling the native grasses, surrounding the village with its dense green coils. The government then stepped in and built a high wall—which, in Corbett's view, "merely freed the villagers from the necessity of erecting fences and watching their crops and gave them more time to devote to the killing of game."

The numbers of deer declined so rapidly that tigers and leopards were forced to fall back on the next best thing: village cattle. When Corbett happened to camp nearby in the spring of 1931, he wrote in his magazine, a dozen villagers squatted outside his tent to ask for aid.

One and all had the same tale to tell. A tiger had taken up its quarters in the lantana and in the course of two years had killed 150 cattle and unless it was destroyed the village would have to be abandoned. While the men were pouring out their tale of woe I observed a pair of vultures circling low over a narrow stretch of lantana running between the village wall and the public road. The two vultures were soon joined by others; so picking up a rifle I set off to investigate. Progress through the lantana was difficult but with the aid of a good hunting knife a way was eventually cut and the remains of a horse killed the previous day found. There were plenty of pug marks around the kill, little of which remained, and it was easy to locate the tiger from his low, continuous growling but impossible to see him in the dense cover.

Returning to the road which was only 40 yards from the kill and little used at this time of the year, I concealed myself behind a bush in the hope that the tiger would follow me to see if I had left the locality, quite a natural thing for it to do. Half an hour later the tiger walked out on to the road and gave me an easy shot as he stood facing me. That evening after I had skinned the tiger—he was a very old animal and I took four bullets and nine pellets of buck shot out of him—I called the villagers together and made an appeal to them on behalf of

*Pages 56–57:*
*The Ramganga River at sunrise, twisting through Corbett National Park in Uttar Pradesh.*

the few remaining deer in the jungle. On the opposite side of the village from my camp, irrigation water had been allowed to flow into the jungle. Over this water *machans* [shooting platforms] had been built in the trees and in these *machans* men sat through the heat of the day, and all night on moon-lit nights, and shot down animals that came to drink. There was no other water within miles and if a thirst-maddened animal avoided one *machan*, it fell victim to the man in the next. I told the villagers that God had given water free for all, and that it was a shameful thing for a man to sit over the water God had provided and shoot His creatures when they came to drink. To do this was to lower themselves below a corpse-eating hyena, for even he, lowest of all creation, did not lie in wait to kill defenseless animals while they were drinking. The men listened to me in silence and when I had done, said they had not looked at the matter in this light, and they promised they would take down the *machans* they had erected and in future would not molest the animals that came to the vicinity of the village to drink. I stayed in the vicinity for several weeks . . . and am glad to say the men kept their promise. I believe that much of the slaughter of deer that is daily taking place . . . would cease if an appeal was made to the better feelings of men. . . .

Corbett appealed to the better feelings of the British government, too. For him, the follies of Indian villagers were to be expected, but those committed by the Raj itself were inexcusable:

It is asserted that in recent years tigers have increased. With this assertion I do not agree. It is a fact that more cattle are being killed every year, this is not due to the tigers having increased but due to the balance of nature having been disturbed by the unrestricted slaughter of game, and also to some extent to tigers having been driven out of their natural haunts where they were seldom or never seen by man, by the activities of the Forest Department. A country's fauna is a sacred trust, and I appeal to you not to betray your trust. Shooting over water, shooting over saltlicks, natural or artificial, shooting birds in the closed-season and when roosting at night, encouraging permit-holders to shoot hinds, fencing off of large areas of forest and the extermination by the Forest Department of all game within these areas, making of unnecessary motor tracks through the forest and shooting from motor cars, absence of sanctuaries and the burning of the forests by the Forest Department and by villagers at a time when the forests are full of young life are all combining to one end—the extermination of our fauna. If we do not bestir ourselves now, it will be to our discredit that the fauna of our province was exterminated in a generation and under our very eyes, while we looked on and never raised a finger to prevent it.

By the mid-thirties, Corbett had himself almost entirely abandoned hunting. A clergyman who knew him only slightly claimed that his conversion came after having been sickened during a duck shoot in which three hundred birds were killed, but no such epiphany was really necessary. It was the solitude of the jungle and what Corbett called his "knowledge of the language and habits of the jungle folk" that had always drawn him, not the shooting. In his later years he rarely fired at anything larger than the red and orange jungle fowl that scratched along the paths near Kaladhungi; when villagers appealed to him to shoot the occasional tiger or leopard

*Above:* Chital move warily through the sunlit Corbett forest.
*Left:* Oblivious to the camera, a male tiger charges toward a herd of sambar at Ranthambhore.

that had taken one of their stray animals, he now refused, paying compensation instead out of his own pocket.

Elsewhere in the Himalayan foothills, a forest officer named F. W. Champion had also gradually abandoned shooting in favor of stalking with a reflex camera, managing finally to capture even the elusive tiger in a series of memorable images published in his pioneering work, *With a Camera in Tiger-Land,* in 1927.

Perhaps in part inspired by Champion, who was a friend and Naini Tal neighbor, Corbett became fascinated with the challenge of capturing tigers on motion picture film. A friend recalled chancing upon Corbett as he stumbled out of a thicket not far from his summer home: "He explained that he had been trying to get a picture of a tigress, but she was in bad temper and as often as he went into the thicket she drove him out. He added however, as one who was ready to make due allowances, that she had her cubs with her." He rarely bothered to carry a rifle during these encounters, hoping instead that he might distract an angry tiger by tossing at it the small khaki pillow on which he sat. When the whir of his camera scared off his subjects, he dammed a stream so that its gurgle would disguise the camera's grinding, then sat day after day for four months in a nearby tree until he was finally able to film seven tigers there at once.

Corbett was sixty-four years old when World War II began, far too old for active service. But he volunteered to recruit an Indian labor corps and later to train British officers and enlisted men in the techniques of jungle survival they would need if they were to win Burma back from the Japanese. The strain finally told: Corbett was ravaged by tick typhus and malaria and by pneumonia that permanently affected his lungs. His weight fell from 175 to 108 pounds, and for a time it seemed unlikely that he would ever walk again, let alone reenter his beloved forests. He spent two years out of action, and perhaps in part just to fill the empty hours began to write the book that became *Man-Eaters of Kumaon.*

His idea was that profits from a modest sale of the book would benefit Indian soldiers blinded in the service of the Crown. Instead, it became an international bestseller, translated into twenty-seven languages and almost universally admired by critics. (Edmund Wilson was a lonely dissenter; Corbett's style, he said, reminded him of "ruptured Kipling.")

Part of the power of Corbett's writing lies in the sometimes maddening faithfulness with which he recalls and recreates the smallest details of his hunts. Above all, he wants his reader to know *just* how it was, no matter how long it takes to describe. The result is the kind of suspense that a professional writer, trained to be more selective, could not easily create.

In the chapter devoted to "The Chowgarh Tigers" in *Man-Eaters of Kumaon,* for example, he takes forty-odd pages to recount his two-year search for a tigress which, with her cub, had killed at least sixty-four people. Along the way he digresses to tell of encounters with mountain goats, a leopard, several tigers, and a bear, and to confess that, in mistakenly shooting the cub rather than the mother while sitting up over a kill, he inadvertently caused the deaths of an additional dozen human victims.

On the nineteenth straight day of stalking, he scrambles down a stony hillside, nearly every inch of which he describes, then lands soundlessly in a sandy streambed at the foot of a tall, sheer rock. Here he details what happened next:

As I stepped clear of the giant slate, I looked behind me over my right shoulder and—looked straight into the tigress's face.

I would like you to have a clear picture of the situation.

The sandy bed behind the rock was quite flat. To the right of it was smooth slate fifteen feet high and leaning slightly outwards, to the left of it was a scoured-out steep bank also some fifteen feet high overhung by a dense tangle of thorn bushes, while at the far end was a slide similar to but a little higher than the one I had glissaded down. The sandy bed enclosed by these three natural walls was about twenty feet long and half as wide, and lying on it, with her forepaws stretched out and her hind legs well tucked under her, was the tigress. Her head, which was raised a few inches off her paws, was eight feet (measured later) from me, and on her face was a smile, similar to that one sees on the face of a dog welcoming his master home from a long absence.

Two thoughts flashed through my mind: one, that it was up to me to make the first move, and the other, that the move would have to be made in such a manner as not to alarm the tigress or make her nervous.

The rifle was in my right hand held diagonally across my chest [Corbett was carrying a clutch of nightjar eggs in his left, found on his way down the hill], with the safety-catch off, and in order to get it to bear on the tigress the muzzle would have to be swung round three-quarters of a circle.

The movement of swinging round the rifle, with one hand, was begun very slowly and hardly perceptibly, and when a quarter of a circle had been made, the stock came in contact with my right side. It was now necessary to extend my arm, and as the stock cleared my side, the swing was very slowly continued. My arm was now at full stretch and the weight of the rifle was beginning to tell. Only a little further now for the muzzle to go, and the tigress—who had not once taken her eyes off mine—was still looking up at me with the pleased expression still on her face.

How long it took the rifle to make the three-quarter circle, I am not in a position to say. To me, looking into the tigress's eyes and unable therefore to follow the movement of the barrel, it appeared that my arm was paralyzed, and that the swing would never be completed. However, the movement was completed at last, and as soon as the rifle was pointing at the tiger's body, I pressed the trigger.

I heard the report, exaggerated in that restricted space, and felt the jar of the recoil, and but for these tangible proofs that the rifle had gone off, I might, for all the immediate result the shot produced, have been in the grip of one of those awful nightmares in which triggers are vainly pulled of rifles that refuse to be discharged at the critical moment.

For a perceptible fraction of time, the tigress remained perfectly still, and then, very slowly, her head sank on to her outstretched paws.

He had, of course, hit his quarry in the heart.

Corbett's publisher, R. E. Hawkins of the Oxford University Press, later theorized that the book's success owed a good deal to its appearance in 1944: "The end of the war was in sight. Years of massive, indiscriminate slaughter and regimentation had eroded faith in the significance of the individual. It was immensely refreshing to read of this contemporary dragon-killer, who in perfect freedom roamed the countryside cheerfully facing danger and hardship to rid the world of tigers and leopards convicted of man-eating. Sir Galahad rode again. Truth and justice had returned."

To be sure, there were those who found some of Corbett's hunting stories hard to credit, and it is true that he did like to tell tall tales, at least when small children were present. He once told his niece, Dorothy Lincoln-Gordon, the following story:

Supposedly, a tiger killed and ate a *dak*-runner, one of the intrepid post office employees who then jogged through the jungles carrying letters, money orders, and the like, their only protection a tall staff hung with bells that announced their presence. A few days later, a nervous substitute jangled along the same path and was also killed. Postal officials then sent two runners along the path at once, instructing them to talk loudly as they passed through the tiger's domain. That seemed to do the trick, and for several weeks all went well—so well that their superintendent thought it safe to return to dispatching a single runner. The tiger took him from the path.

"Uncle Jim was contacted and asked to help," his niece recalled being told. "He decided to be the runner and set out for the forest, carrying the [staff] with its bells and his rifle. He went jingling through and as he rounded the bend there was the tiger, waiting for him, but before it could spring, he'd dropped the [staff], raised the rifle and shot it."

Perhaps wisely, Corbett never committed this uncharacteristically gaudy story to paper. And when he did recount his adventures, he bent over backward to be self-deprecating, carefully cataloguing his own weaknesses, documenting every wrong path taken, every missed shot and loudly snapping twig.

Beyond the tales of Corbett's quests lies an extraordinary body of accurately observed detail about life in the Indian jungles in general and the behavior of tigers in particular. (This last, Corbett admitted, was mostly gleaned after he had given up

A tiger's fangs are formidable-looking weapons even when exposed only in a yawn.

the rifle for the camera.) Most of his independent findings have been borne out by subsequent scientists: Tigers kill with their teeth, not their paws. They do so as readily in broad daylight as they do in darkness, provided they are left undisturbed by human beings. A man-eater "is a tiger that has been compelled, through stress of circumstances beyond its control to a diet alien to it," and "stress is, in nine cases out of ten, wounds, and in the tenth case, old age."

He did all that he could to deflate the myth that the tiger was man's natural enemy. "The author who first used the words 'as cruel as a tiger' and 'as bloodthirsty as a tiger' when attempting to emphasize the evil character of the villain of his piece," he wrote in the opening pages of *Man-Eaters of Kumaon*, "not only showed lamentable ignorance of the animal he defamed, but coined phrases which have come into universal circulation, and which are mainly responsible for the wrong opinion of tigers held by all except the small proportion of the public who have the opportunity of forming their own opinions."

Sadly, however, the final impact of Corbett's writing on the larger public was probably the opposite of what he intended. What we remember best from his books are the harrowing details of long nights spent sitting up over corpses; the dread of the grieving villagers huddled in their huts; the astonishing strength and tenacity of even the most apparently enfeebled man-eaters, which again and again Corbett had to track down after inflicting fearful wounds.

In this gory context, his pleas for understanding his powerful, stealthy quarry tended to be forgotten; his repeated warnings that the species would soon disappear unless drastic action was taken fell mostly on deaf ears.

In 1946, Corbett tried to warn the Viceroy himself of what he feared was coming. "He has rather pessimistic views on the future of tigers," Lord Wavell noted in his journal; "he put the present tiger population of India at 3,000 to 4,000 (I was rather surprised at the smallness of this estimate) and that in many parts of India tigers will become almost extinct in the next 10 or 15 years; his chief reason is that Indian politicians are no sportsmen and tigers have no votes, while the right to a gun licence will go with a vote."

Indian independence finally came in 1947. Corbett was certain it spelled disaster. The Indians were still incapable of governing themselves; that had been the central premise of the Raj, and of Corbett's own beliefs. His beloved forests would now be razed or overrun; wildlife would be obliterated; Hailey Park was doomed. Finally, he was sure, once the British had gone, the Soviets would march down through his mountains to seize the subcontinent. His sister Maggie, now seventy-two, had still more immediate fears: The Indians were sure to wreak an awful vengeance on any Britons who dared remain behind, raping and burning and killing as she had been told they had done in her grandparents' time. They must flee.

The Corbetts sold their houses at Naini Tal and Kaladhungi. But where were they to go? India had been their family home for at least three generations. Corbett had only visited Britain briefly once in his life. Instead, they withdrew to the White Highlands of Kenya, where British settlers, including several of their relatives, still struggled to hold on to something of the old imperial life. They rented a cottage in the garden of the Outspan Hotel at Nyeri. It had once been occupied by that earlier model of British sportsmanship, Lord Baden-Powell, the founder of Scouting. Here, the aging Corbett spent his last years, filming lions and elephants whenever he felt strong enough, feeding the twenty-six varieties of birds that fluttered in and out of the garden, and tapping out with one finger five more books—*The Man-Eating Leopard of Rudraprayag* (1948), *My India* (1952), *Jungle Lore* (1953), *The Temple Tiger and More Man-Eaters of Kumaon* (1954), and *Tree Tops* (1955)—tearing out a page and starting over whenever he made a mistake. He wrote back to India often, too, inquiring about the mustard crop at Kaladhungi, wanting reassurance that his house was being properly cared for by its new owners, hinting that he might come back for a visit.

Kenya provided precious little sanctuary. The thin Highlands air did not agree with Corbett and his weakened lungs steadily weakened further, but he refused even to think of moving again. "One has to live *somewhere,*" he told Maggie. The Mau Mau rebellion had begun. Maggie found a Kikuyu hidden beneath her bed one evening when her brother was away. The intruder demanded money; she refused to give him any and was knocked down as he fled.

In February 1952 Princess Elizabeth and Prince Philip visited Kenya and requested that when they spent a night at Tree Tops—a lushly appointed game-watching hut built high in the branches of an ancient ficus tree overlooking a busy waterhole—Corbett act as their guide. The twenty hours he spent there in the company of royalty was Corbett's "day of days," he wrote, more important and more filled with meaning for the old country-bottled colonial than any of the deeds for which the rest of the world remembered him. Proximity to the princess made him gush: her face was "as fresh as a flower, no artificial aids were needed or used to enhance the bloom of her cheeks." Her approach to Tree Tops, an uneventful stroll past trumpeting but distant elephants, he pronounced one of the "most courageous acts" he had ever witnessed. He was permitted to hold her camera and pocketbook as she climbed the ladder, and later he sat between the princess and the prince at dinner.

After the royal couple had gone to bed, he spent the rest of the night as he had spent so many others, in the open, sitting motionless, rifle across his lap, watching not for a tiger or a leopard this time, but for terrorists. None appeared, but that same night George VI died suddenly in London, making his daughter monarch of the

Jim Corbett enjoys a cigarette at the old Dikhala Rest House, now the center of a crowded tourist complex in the heart of Corbett Park.

retreating Empire. "When I helped her into the tree she was a princess," he marveled to a friend a few days later, "and when I helped her down she was a queen."

Jim Corbett died of a heart attack on April 19, 1955, and was buried in the tiny Anglican cemetery at Nyeri, 3,500 miles from his real home.

"In the olden days," Corbett's old friend, Lord Hailey, wrote after his death, "he would have been one of the small band of Europeans whose memory has been worshipped by Indians as that of men who were in some measure also gods." Hailey's words, like so many of Corbett's own, were tinged with affectionate condescension, but certainly in India more than most places specifics do seem to fade with time, distinctions blur, the secular somehow becomes sanctified. A young man from Kanda, a hilltop village near which Corbett shot one of his last man-eaters, has trouble now remembering just what his grandfather had told him of the shooting. Had the tiger killed three people before Corbett came, or was it six? "Carpet-sahib was god," the aged headman of another village explained to an interviewer a few years ago. "The goddess appeared to him in person."

Corbett's old home at Kaladhungi has been transformed into a museum by the Forest Department of Uttar Pradesh, and its former owner's new aura of sanctity is evident everywhere among the sparse exhibits. There are not many visitors; a new road to Naini Tal has been built, and so there is no need for most travelers to pass the garden gate as they once did. Five uniformed forest officers were therefore free to accompany me through the bungalow's three small rooms one morning in the winter of 1986. Around the stained walls are hung brief passages from Corbett's writings: *Any task well accomplished gives pleasure; From November to March the climate of the Himalayan foothills has no equal; The knowledge you absorb today will be added to the knowledge you will absorb tomorrow.* Unexceptional statements, but each reverently hand-lettered as if it were sacred scripture. Corbett's posthumous sainthood may owe something to the fact that he never married; Hindu sages are traditionally celibate. "Jim Corbett *bachelor*," one of the forest officers eagerly assured me. "Sister Maggie bachelor, too."

I was shown several relics, including Corbett's folding steel campbed, a big clumsy affair which I was solemnly assured had been the platform from which he shot his tigers; his crabapple walking stick, taken down from the old gun case in which it is kept for me to hold for a moment; and a cracked white cup from which he sipped his morning tea in Kenya. The officer in charge fished into a grimy creased envelope and brought out between thumb and forefinger a single guinea-fowl feather; Corbett was said to have given it to a friend a month before he died.

There have been a lot of changes since Corbett's day. Hailey Park, whose survival Corbett worried over, was renamed Corbett Park after his death; it is now nearly twice its former size and a favorite site for visitors hoping to see a tiger.

Trucks blare past the Kaladhungi compound these days, and tractors plow the fields that Corbett's villagers worked with bullocks. But their thatch huts are still engulfed in green wheat; mangoes still ripen in the old hunter's garden; the spotted deer still steal down out of the forest to drink in the evening. And just at sunset one day not long before my visit, a tiger was seen sitting in the dry bed of the Baur River, not far from where Jim Corbett saw the pug marks of his first tigers more than a century ago.

How long tigers will still be seen there is anybody's guess.

## CHAPTER FOUR

# THE PRESIDING DEITY

Morning comes early at Tiger Haven. Before there is enough light to see the time, the jungle fowl begin to crow, big drops of dew patter among the brittle sal leaves on the forest floor behind the house, and through the ceiling of our room comes a steady clanking: Billy Arjan Singh, in his seventies, is lifting weights on the upstairs verandah.

A few minutes later his voice is heard, calling, *"Ah! Ah! (Come! Come!),"* and if you pad to the window, pull back the brightly printed curtain and wipe the condensation from the glass, you can see him standing on the verandah in the morning mist, thick legs set wide apart, wearing a knitted cap, shaggy sweater and khaki shorts, tearing off small bits of *chapati* and flinging them to a dozen cawing jungle crows, several rock pigeons, and a hungry peacock which acts like a pet chicken because that is what it thinks it is. It was hatched by a hen from an egg Billy found abandoned in the forest, and it has lived all its life among the barnyard fowl that scratch across his lawn; the far-off siren calls of wild peafowl seem only to bewilder this huge shimmering chicken, its long neck stretched eagerly toward its master.

The line between wild and tame, man and animal, has always been blurred at Tiger Haven. Billy raised three leopards and a tigress here, and released them all into the Dudhwa National Park that starts just across the narrow Neora River behind his house, the park that he himself carved out single-handedly and still tries to guard against all its enemies, internal and external. Those enemies include hunters and poachers, farmers and woodgatherers, corrupt policemen and venal politicians—and some officials of the Forest Department who ought by rights to be his allies.

When I first met him in 1987, he was nearly seventy; the big cats were all gone from his house—though photographs of them covered the walls and spilled over onto tables and bookshelves and mantelpieces—and most of his battles should have been behind him. That they were not—that he would in fact soon find himself hounded and harassed by his own state government—is testimony both to the precariousness of the conservation cause in India for which he has fought for most of his adult life, and to the flinty integrity of his character.

Why, I once asked him, did he so stubbornly stay on in the forest? Tiger Haven is more than eleven hours by road from Delhi, after all, without a telephone or reliable electricity, murderously hot in the summer, subject to spring floods that confine him to the upper story of his house for days at a time.

"I'm the presiding deity here," he answered softly. "Everyone comes. Everyone goes. But I remain." He has remained, presiding, for nearly half a century.

Indomitable, incorruptible—and sometimes impossible—Billy Arjan Singh represents not only another time but another India. To know Billy is to glimpse life as it was for a chosen few under the British Raj. To begin with, he is of noble blood—he is still formally addressed as *Kanwar* (Prince) Arjan Singh ("Billy" is a boyhood nickname)—a descendant of the Sikh rulers of Kapurthala State in the Punjab. His great-grandfather was Raja Randhir Singh, who rallied to the British during the 1857

*Opposite:* A massive male tiger at Kanha.

Mutiny, helped lift the siege of Lucknow, and was rewarded for his help with a knighthood and vast holdings of land in what is now Uttar Pradesh.

Randhir Singh had two sons. When the eldest, who ascended to the throne at his father's death, failed to provide his kingdom with a son and died young, the throne should have passed to his younger brother (and Billy's great-grandfather), Harnam Singh. But, if family tradition is to be believed, someone bribed the British Resident and Civil Surgeon to back the false claim of the late Maharaja's widow that she had been pregnant at the time of his death. A baby was then smuggled into the palace, and solemnly declared the rightful heir. He grew to be enormously fat and famously fond of foreign women—one of them, a Czech dancer, jumped or was pushed to her death from the top of the Qutb Minar at Delhi—but he is best remembered for the fascination with all things French that led him to build a miniature Versailles at Kapurthala, complete with gilt ceilings, formal gardens and chefs trained in Paris.

Harnam Singh repeatedly petitioned the government of India to be restored to the throne he stubbornly insisted was his; but, according to Billy, even after the Maharani made a deathbed confession that she had never been pregnant, the British did not dare reverse themselves for fear of revealing the venality of their officials. Instead, they knighted Harnam Singh and saw to it that he was given charge of all the family lands in U.P. Now Raja Sir Harnam Singh, he fell under a missionary's spell and became a Christian, a conversion which may have improved his prospects in the hereafter but dimmed them in the here and now, for it ensured that neither he nor his descendants would ever be allowed to rule: the British, ever fearful of injuring any-one's religious sensibilities and thereby causing a repetition of the 1857 uprising, would not hear of imposing a Christian prince upon a Sikh state.

Billy is very amusing about the trials and pretensions of his royal ancestors, but to ride with him in his Land Rover is to see just how long-lasting are the assumptions of princely India: he hums along at a steady pace, both big hands on the wheel, and when faced with any of the obstacles that make driving in India so maddening—wall-eyed water buffalo lumbering onto the road, a herd of oblivious goats filling it from side to side, even an overloaded truck, sounding its brassy horn and bearing directly down on him—he merely lifts one hand slightly, gestures toward the side of the road, and keeps going. Somehow, a way is always made for him to pass.

Perhaps understandably, Sir Harnam Singh does not seem to have been a happy man; according to his grandson, his huge dark eyes were often bloodshot from the whiskey with which he filled his evenings, and he had a fearful temper. But his chil-dren went on to distinguish themselves: One son became a High Court judge at Lahore and was knighted; another was a celebrated cricketer and soldier; and his daughter, Rajkumari Amrit Kaur (whom Billy and his siblings called "Aunt B"), was head girl at her British boarding school before becoming a prominent disciple of Mahatma Gandhi and, later, the first Minister of Health in the government of inde-pendent India.

Billy's father, Jasbir Singh, was the youngest of the children and rose the highest within the Raj. Gregarious, charming and a fine athlete, despite his short, stocky frame—good at tennis, hockey, soccer, cricket, golf, pig-sticking, bird shooting—he attended Balliol College at Oxford, then returned to India and went into the British Provincial Service. "I'm an Indian and must identify with Indian independence," he would tell his children, but, he believed, it was up to people like him slowly to pre-pare the country for freedom.

In 1914, he married the daughter of an English woman and an Indian Deputy Inspector of Police, Mabel Golaknath. She was a formidable young woman, erudite and well traveled, with a degree in education from the University of Indiana. There would be four children. The first son, Jaswant, was born the following year.

Billy. was born in Gorakhpur, in what was then called the United Provinces, on August 15, 1917, and raised in the princely state of Balrampur, where for nine years his father served as the Special Manager for the nominal ruler of the state, then still a minor and, according to Billy, none too bright.

"Our aunts and uncles thought Billy the most beautiful thing they'd ever seen," his younger sister, Amar, remembers being told. "Fat and fair. Up to two. Then, suddenly, he couldn't keep his food down. Grew thin and frail." He became so ill, his mother remembered, that for a time he forgot how to talk. She feared for his life, made sure that he was "cocooned and closeted" by the servants, kept him from other children and out of school. There were tutors to teach him his lessons, governesses to teach him manners and British adventure books to stir his imagination: H. Rider Haggard, Sir Arthur Conan Doyle, Rudyard Kipling, whose "Here's to You, Fuzzy Wuzzy" Billy can still recite without a pause.

"Our father rather emphasized strength," his sister recalls, and he had hoped to pass on his love of sport to his sons. He delighted in Jaswant's prowess at games but despaired of Billy. "I was a poor also-ran who didn't cut much ice anywhere," Billy remembered, and he drew close to his mother: In a battered album at Tiger Haven there is a large sepia photograph of a gathering of the big Kapurthala clan. Thin and large-eyed, Billy huddles close to his mother's feet, in vivid contrast to his chubby older brother, who sits with his head cocked back and his chest puffed out, serenely self-assured.

One evening when Billy was eight and so ill that his parents did not dare leave home to dine with a British physician, the doctor asked if he could see the boy, took one look and prescribed an elixir which began what seems to have been an almost

Billy Arjan Singh and his first tiger, shot in the forests of Balrampur.

miraculous recovery. Billy remembers the medicine as "Paratythroid"; his sister believes it was some sort of calcium compound. Whatever it was, without it Billy would almost certainly have died.

Billy never quite caught up with himself, never made up for those missing years. Somehow, he once told me, he has always felt "odd man out." His illness was not the only thing that set him apart. In a family that prized after-dinner repartee, he was reticent and shy. His father was so fine a bass that his sons gathered around him as he sat in his tin tub taking his morning bath, just to watch him shave and hear him sing "Ol' Man River" and "Carry Me Back to Old Virginny" amid the steam. Both of Billy's brothers inherited something of their father's deep, rich voice, but Billy's, damaged by his childhood illness and a botched tonsillectomy, is high and unsteady, his words sometimes indistinct. "I *hate* my voice," he says. There is a good deal about himself he seems to dislike, for if he has found wanting most of the human beings who have passed through his life, he finds himself the most wanting of all.

As soon as he regained his feet, his sister says, he retreated into the forest. Outshone as a small boy by his magnetic older brother and now perhaps threatened by the advent of two more siblings—Amar, seven years younger than he, and a second brother, Balram, nine years younger—he found solace and an outlet for his anger shooting animals and birds with an air rifle. Frogs and gecko lizards were favorite targets; so were songbirds. His early enthusiasm for shooting still bothers him: "My brother [Jaswant] never displayed this compulsive instinct for slaughter," he has written, "and I can only conjecture that he had wider interests and more satisfying talents which prevented him from indulging in these mindless orgies of destruction to prove himself." But no such rueful thoughts then nagged at him: When Amar and Balram tried to toddle after him, he would aim his weapon at them. The forest was *his* world—and only his. It is an attitude to which he has clung all his life.

Everything about the life Billy's family lived at Balrampur suggested that he was a privileged person to whom the rules governing others need not apply. His father was the real ruler of the state, "the king by proxy," Billy says. An army of three hundred soldiers answered to his orders; one hundred elephants were his to command. When the slack-jawed Maharaja was helped onto the royal elephant for the *Dussehra* procession that marked the high point of the Hindu year, Jasbir Singh, wearing a large turban and a crisply tailored suit, rode next to him in his howdah. And his sons basked in their father's reflected glory: When Billy and a friend decided to take their air rifles to the local zoo after hours so that they could pepper its helpless incarcerated animals with pellets, the zoo director dared do nothing to stop them; and there was no one to object when Jasbir Singh took his boys into the Balrampur forests on the edge of the terai, riding in an open Cadillac as part of a dusty flotilla of princely vehicles, firing at everything and anything that moved. Billy shot his first leopard at twelve, his first tiger at fourteen, and when the family summered at Naini Tal—where Billy and his siblings rode in a *dandy* carried by four coolies—Jim Corbett himself, a friend of Billy's father, regaled him every Sunday morning with tales of tiger shooting.

In 1932, the Balrampur idyll abruptly ended. Sir Malcolm Hailey, the governor of the United Provinces and Corbett's old shooting companion, was anxious for diplomatic reasons that a marriage be arranged between Balrampur's weak-minded prince and the bright and attractive daughter of the commander-in-chief of the neighboring kingdom of Nepal. Jasbir Singh was adamantly against it. "Why do you want to ruin the life of a pretty girl by marrying her to this impotent boy?" he asked—and was summarily transferred for questioning the orders of his superior. It was a blow to the family's sense of British fairness, and Jasbir took a year's leave to get over it.

Billy was fifteen and had still never attended school. Jaswant had been sent off to the Prince of Wales Royal Indian Military College at Dehra Dun at the age of eleven, the start of what would be a distinguished military career. But the memory of Billy's illness and concern that it might somehow recur evidently made his parents hesitate to be apart from him, and when they finally decided to enroll him in Philander Smith College at Naini Tal he was to board in the home of the headmaster rather than live alongside the other boys. "I was in the school but not of it," Billy remembers. He cannot have been an easy guest; he insisted on keeping a vicious monkey on a rope, built himself a hide of branches and thatch in the forest behind the house in which to do his studying, and discovered Charles Atlas and became obsessed with weightlifting. When, during a visit home, his mother asked him why on earth he was still at it long after midnight, he answered, "God gave Jaswant everything. He gave me nothing. So I have to do it myself." Through hard work he transformed himself from a frail, slender schoolboy into a massively muscled young man.

He did well at Philander Smith, but failed at Lucknow Christian College, thereby greatly annoying his father, just squeaked through Meerut and Allahabad universities, then failed an examination to become an officer in the Indian Police—in part, he suspects, because when asked for the name of his favorite author, he replied, "P. G. Wodehouse," not the sort of reading favored by the Indian constabulary. Again, Jasbir Singh was disappointed.

But he did not give up on his second son, and when World War II began in 1939, he persuaded a British brigadier and old friend to help get Billy an emergency commission as a second lieutenant in the First Indian Field Regiment of Artillery.

Army life did not suit Billy. He enjoyed the rugged physical training, but there was little room for the animals that remained his first love. He kept a goat in his barracks room for a time, according to his sister, then adopted a mongoose, which he named "Rikki" after Kipling's "Rikki Tikki Tavi" and encouraged to sleep in his left boot. One morning, when he appeared on the parade ground wearing one boot and shoe and explaining that his other boot was otherwise occupied, he was ordered to get rid of the animal. He handed it over to his orderly, then took it back surreptitiously when the mongoose could not be dissuaded from shadowing the man wherever he went, nipping at his bare heels. His sister no longer recalls what finally happened to Rikki, but as she told me the story, I suddenly remembered Billy once ruefully telling me that the problem with keeping a mongoose as a pet was that it was too easily stepped upon. Perhaps Rikki met his end beneath one of Billy's big Army boots.

In any case, animals were not his biggest problem in the Army; human beings were, as they would be throughout his life. "I would have liked the Army but got into bad company," he later recalled. He enjoyed gunnery school at Kakul in what is now Pakistan, liked zeroing in the howitzers, then watching as they spewed tracers toward the target and hurled debris up from the pocked hillsides across the valley. But he disliked taking orders from anyone, could not abide military bureaucracy, and soon got into trouble again. Told verbally he could go home on leave, he left camp only to discover that permission in writing had been required. When he returned, he

was given a severe dressing down. To Billy, his superior's word should have been enough. Other soldiers more zealously nationalistic than he encouraged him to believe that he was being singled out for harsh treatment because he was an Indian. "We began discussing the bad traits of the white man," he remembers now, and "I became uppish with the British officers."

Finally, he appealed directly to the brigadier who had helped get him his commission, asking for transfer to another unit where he would be treated more fairly. The brigadier was evidently appalled at his presumption, and Billy was placed on "adverse report," unfit for active service. When the First Field Artillery finally sailed for action in Burma, Billy was made to stay behind in India, first with one anti-tank unit and then, when it too moved toward the front, held back again and assigned to another. Finally, he got orders to accompany the Fifth Mahratta Anti-Tank Regiment to the Middle East.

His father saw him off at the Lucknow railroad station. "Do your best," he said. "I know you will never falter or fail." Billy never faltered, but he did fail. Jasbir Singh died of typhoid fever a few months after his second son shipped out, and so did not live to see it—or to witness the unique triumphs that were his once the war had ended.

He spent more than a year in Persia. Three times the guns were readied for action and three times withdrawn. Otherwise, there was little to do but endure the searing daytime heat and freezing desert nights. Finally, the regiment was brought back to India, to the flyblown cantonment town of Ranchi.

Billy was miserable there. "I did not get on with my Commanding Officer," he remembered, "nor did I care for the men I served with, and what rankled was that the predicament was my fault." Cheated of the opportunity to distinguish himself in combat, as Jaswant had done, guilt-stricken that he had once again failed to live up to his late father's expectations for him, he fell ill with malaria, and when his colonel, a man named Gurney, accused him of malingering, he rose from his bed in a fury and warned that if the man said anything like that again, he'd break his face.

Gurney reported him. Billy asked to be transferred to the Air Force, where Jaswant was now a squadron commander. The request was denied: Billy was given the choice of resigning or being cashiered.

He resigned. He was twenty-eight years old and had no idea what to do with himself.

"Up to then my life was a total failure," he told me; his efforts to make his own way outside the charmed circle of his family had ended in defeat. He made a desultory attempt at finding a job in business as his younger brother Balram had done, but found nothing. Then, he chanced to pay a visit to an old friend, the younger brother of a petty prince who had begun farming on the edge of the *terai* in Kheri District, not far from the town of Palia Kalan—a still scruffier crossroads then than it is now, but grandly called "Greater Palia" nonetheless.

The town had little charm; but for someone as fond of the solitude the forest affords as Billy, the surrounding landscape was a revelation. Swamps and grass-lands spread out in all directions, filled with game. Across the plain to the north, reserved forest ran unbroken to the border with Nepal. The appeal of living and working in the midst of this sportsman's paradise was irresistible: "It seemed to me that all the frustrations I had felt ... were worthwhile if I could earn my living in such surroundings."

Billy picked out and purchased 750 acres, and named his farm "Jasbirnagar" for the father whose legacy had made its purchase possible. He described his arrival in *The Legend of the Maneater*, the fifth book he has written about his experiences.

I was on the passenger train from Lucknow, where my mother had now bought a house ... [and pulled in] at 3:30 in the morning. A small bullock cart ... was waiting for me and as it was a moonlit night, I loaded my luggage onto it before setting off on the three-mile walk along the dirt track road which led to my farm site.... The track was deeply rutted, and ankle deep in dust, but the stars shone brightly, and a waning moon lit the twin ribbons ahead. To the north an Indian fox gave a chattering bark, while in the copse a pack of jackals sang their eerie falsetto chorus: "Dead Hindu. Dead Hindu. Where are you? Where are you? Heer, Heeer."

The sky was paling as I approached Jasbirnagar, which was what I had decided to call my farm, and further on a hog deer fled with consecutive piping whistles of alarm. The sawing grunts of a leopard as it retired to its lair indicated what had frightened the deer. As I turned into my land, a vista of grassland stretched endlessly to the West. A herd of twenty nilghai stood in an opening ... and further on a large herd of black buck cropped the short Imperata grass. The herds of numerous cattle, both cows and buffaloes, glinted in the light of the dawn. In front of me lay most of what I would have to contend with if I was going to make a success of farming.

Billy built himself a thatched hut in which he would live year-round for nine years, and went to work carving a farm out of a wilderness. He knew nothing about agriculture when he began; the whole region was malarial and infested with gangs of *dacoits* (bandits); deer, wild boar and domestic cattle devoured his crops almost as soon as he got them into the ground. But with the same dogged determination with which he had remade himself physically, he imposed himself on his land, shooting the pigs that destroyed his barley and wheat, paddy and sugar cane; standing guard against the bandits; driving off the cattle—and the Muslim graziers who owned them—finally building himself a modest white-washed house.

It was a lonely life, for although Billy paid court to several women, including the daughter of a prominent political family, in the end he could persuade none to accept a life so far from civilization and its comforts. Still, Jasbirnagar had its satisfactions. For the first few years, Billy was the only large-scale farmer in the area, nearly as powerful as his late father had been at Balrampur, and a law unto himself: When stray cattle were found in his fields, he tied them out as bait for tigers as an object lesson to their owners. He may have been more feared than loved by his neighbors, but the surrounding savannah was still alive with deer and antelope. Crocodiles lazed on the banks of the rivers that twisted through the tall grass, and at night tigers and leopards prowled the countryside in search of prey.

But elsewhere in India after independence in 1947, Jim Corbett's worst fears about the fate of India's wildlife seemed about to be borne out. Gun licenses, once reserved for a privileged few, were now made available to any farmer who could afford a firearm. British game laws were gleefully flouted as vestiges of the hated colonial regime. During the day, jeeps full of hunters slammed their way across farmers' fields, banging away at the helpless, dwindling herds of black buck that fled before them. The farmers themselves sat up over water holes in the heat of summer, shooting anything desperate enough to show itself for a drink. The princes were stripped of their old power to bar hunters from their shooting preserves, and under cover of darkness, caravans of cars bristling with guns and equipped with spotlights moved methodically through them, firing at every pair of eyes that glittered in the blackness. And forest officials were paid to look the other way as *shikar* outfitters bent what few rules were left for the sake of foreign clients, many of them Americans, whom the government saw as prime sources of badly needed foreign exchange.

A few concerned citizens saw what was happening, and in 1952 the Indian Board for Wildlife was created to advise the central and state governments on conservation; but in an India still struggling to adjust to independence and faced with so many human problems, its warnings were generally ignored.

The killing went on. The dirty little secret of tiger *shikar* always was that, for all the excitement surrounding it, the actual shooting of a tiger had never been terribly difficult. "Tigers aren't hard to figure out," a jaded old *shikari* once told me. "They only know how to do four things—eat, sleep, hunt and fuck." The tiger rarely moves unseen; the forests ring with the sound of its passing, an angry, terrified chorus of birds and deer and birds and infuriated monkeys that permits even an inexperienced hunter to trace his progress. An American technical expert, stationed in Central India during the mid-1950s, shot two young male tigers by the simple expedient of letting his golden spaniel run ahead of him along the bank of a canal cut through the forest. Apparently, the tigers had never seen such brightly colored, oblivious prey, and as they stalked the cheerful snuffling dog, the hunter cheerfully stalked them.

The American writer and big-game hunter Robert Ruark, who shot three tigers in Madhya Pradesh in 1954, was suitably impressed by his prey but entirely realistic about the ease with which he'd shot it. In *Use Enough Gun*, he wrote:

> A dead tiger is the biggest thing I have ever seen in my life, and I have shot an elephant. A live tiger is the most exciting thing I have ever seen in my life, and I

India's other great predator, the Asiatic lion, is now confined to a single forest, the Gir, in western Gujarat.

Genghis, the big tiger that once reigned over the lakes at Ranthambhore, expresses his unhappiness at having spotted a human intruder.

have shot a lion. A tiger in a hurry is the fastest thing I have ever seen in my life, and I have shot a leopard. A wild tiger is the most frightening thing I have ever seen and I have shot a Cape Buffalo. But for the sport involved … I would rather shoot quail than shoot another tiger.

I am not discounting the fact that if you wait for a driven tiger on the ground or in a pit, or in a tree at night, there is a certain tendency to choke on your heart. Nor do I ignore the trophy value of a tiger, because spread flat on the floor or draped on a wall he will dominate any room. It is just that I would not walk from here to the corner to shoot another tiger. It's too easy....

How anybody misses a tiger I cannot say. He is as big as a Shetland pony.... Shoot him in the neck or head or shoulder, and he's a dead cat [and] unless you see him under fifty yards, you won't see him at all....

Two years later, another well-known but far more gullible American hunter, Jack Denton Scott, the "adventure" columnist for the *New York Herald Tribune,* visited the same region. He was more typical of the foreign *shikaris* who flocked to India after independence.

The number of animals was falling so fast by then—Scott's guide cheerfully professed to have personally dispatched forty tigers and more than one hundred leopards, and to have helped his clients kill two hundred and fifty more big cats—that daytime hunting was no longer profitable. Greedy *shikar* outfitters had hastily evolved a dubious mystique to justify illegal jacklighting—using powerful spotlights to freeze animals in place until even the clumsiest hunter could pot them from the front seat of their jeep—to foreigners in whose countries it had long been outlawed. Jacklighting actually *favored* Indian animals, they claimed, and Scott bought it all:

"… the night is the element of the leopard and the tiger, you are meeting him on an uneven basis," he reported breathlessly in *Forests of the Night*. "He knows the roads, the forests, every ravine…. The light however almost puts us on an equal footing with him. But not quite. These cats are animals that are always hunting, always on the alert. They may be hunting us before we know that we are hunting them." (This last is especially ludicrous; if there is a single instance of a tiger or leopard attacking anyone sitting quietly in a jeep, I have never come across it.)

When he at last dared venture into the forest, Scott was made to live in a state of perpetual terror. One morning, he and his *shikari* got word that a tiger had killed a buffalo bait. They drove together to within half a mile of the kill, then walked toward the site. As they neared the half-eaten buffalo, Scott wrote,

> Suddenly, quietly, Rao touched me on the shoulder and turned his head slightly; his darting brown eyes gave me urgent direction.
>
> There looking above the grass—grass that came to my hips, indicating how enormous he was—stood a black and gold tiger, his straight-up ears twitching. Except for the movement of the ears and a noise he made, he stood sculpturesquely still, fearful symmetry without motion. The noise was a deep *ahhh-hh*, a moan, almost a cough.
>
> Even in that dreadful instant a few classic words from some long-ago classroom flashed across my mind: "Do you know what fear is? No ordinary fear of insult, injury, or death, but abject, quivering dread, a fear that dries the inside of the mouth and half of the throat, fear that makes you sweat on the palms of the hands, and gulp in order to keep the uvula at work. This is fine Fear—a great cowardice, and must be felt to be appreciated…."
>
> I was appreciating it, gulping like a goldfish, and my hands were beaded with sweat.
>
> We were in a lost position, almost a hundred yards from the tree and the safety of the machan. In a few quick bounds the tiger could be among us, sweeping his great paws. It would have to be one shot, and it would have to kill him—dead. Or else we would be. Now, suddenly, the three of us had rifles at our shoulders. It was a long shot, *at least three hundred yards* [my italics] and I had no scope on the .458 and all I could see clearly was his great head…. Now we knew how death in the jungle arrived, silently, deadly, without warning.

It did not arrive, of course; came nowhere near him, in fact. Instead, the tiger moaned his annoyance again—Scott thought it "a bone-chilling sound"—then turned and melted into the grass.

By 1963, when Robert Ruark returned to the jungles of Madhya Pradesh for a second hunt, the game had grown so wary as to be virtually invisible by day. "It is my considered opinion that 90 percent of India's fast vanishing game is shot at night," Ruark wrote then, "on the road, by flashlight, from a moving vehicle…. The visiting American with his dollars has compounded the felony of total lack of sportsmanship on the part of the Indian hunter. The man pays his money and he wants a tiger. The shikar firms will guarantee you a tiger or part of your money back."

Hunting the same territory from which he had taken three tigers on his first visit, Ruark refused to enter the forest after dark: jacklighting was illegal, he said, and, besides, there was no sport in it.

Day followed day without so much as a hint of a big cat. Finally, his increasingly desperate chief *shikari* slipped out of camp for a time one afternoon, then returned for his client late in the evening. If Ruark would just get into the jeep, he said, he would be *guaranteed* a leopard.

"I went along with the gag," Ruark recalled:

At a measured distance from camp, Butt jammed on the brakes. His assistant flashed the lamp and my noble guide said, "There is leopard, Sahib; you are shooting quickly. I am shooting behind you, isn't it?"

I have remarkably good eyes for an old and battered boy, but I could not see any leopard nor could I see any movement for a solid five minutes.

"Why are you not shooting leopard?" said Khan Sahib Jamshed Butt.

"I am not shooting bloody leopard, because I am not being able to *see* bloody leopard, and I am not shooting what I am not seeing, isn't it?"

Ruark demanded to be taken back to camp.

Out early the next morning, he found the leopard, stone dead and propped carefully against a tree. The *shikari* had shot it the previous evening to ensure his client a trophy—and himself a handsome profit.

Still, the damage done even by the unprecedented post-independence fusillade could not compare with that inflicted by the inexorable growth of India's population that accompanied it. When India won its freedom, there were fewer than 500 million people on the whole subcontinent. Now, even with Pakistan and Bangladesh partitioned off, there will soon be one billion people living in India alone.

This human tide continues to wash away the great forests that blanketed almost half the country in 1900. As forests were cleared for commercial planting, cut down or lopped for firewood and thatch, or chewed over by countless head of livestock, that figure would steadily be reduced to less than 15 percent.

More than 1,700 tiger-shooting permits were issued in 1967, but only 168 tigers were actually shot. The targets were disappearing. Two separate studies suggested that there were fewer than two thousand tigers in the whole country. Genuine sportsmen were appalled, and some hunters, wildlife enthusiasts and forest officials alike began to stir themselves and demand an end to the killing.

During Billy Arjan Singh's first years at Jasbirnagar, Kheri District had been largely immune to the slaughter occurring elsewhere in India. But before long, industrious refugees from the Punjab began to push into the region, draining swamps, plowing up the grasslands, planting green walls of sugar cane. The plain surrounding Billy's farm was soon being carved up into fields and dotted with villages whose inhabitants eagerly took part in the same indiscriminate shooting then going on all over the subcontinent. Fewer and fewer animals visited Jasbirnagar. Palia crept closer.

Human society was closing in on Billy once again; he began to feel "smothered by cultivation," and on a hot May morning in 1959—after fourteen years on his farm—he set out on elephant-back toward the Reserved Forest, seven miles to the north, in search of a new, more remote site on which to live.

The spot where we stopped that morning ... had not yet succumbed to the ploughs and harvesters, which had already domesticated most of the savannah on the plain. It was rough scrub land interspersed with single trees growing

here and there, giving it the appearance of a wild park. I walked along the
edge of the forest for a little way, exploring the area, and soon came upon
an open space surrounded by forest on three sides. Standing there, facing
south ... [n]ot a single sign of human life disturbed the view. There were no
electricity pylons, no road, no habitation of any kind. The only reminder of the
outside world was the sound of the trains trundling heavily down the tracks with
their loads of sugar cane, seven miles away, a sound which reinforced one's
sense of isolation....

Behind me was the meeting point of two rivers [one, the Soheli], the other a
shallow and lazy stream called the Neora which flowed down from the hills of
Nepal and meandered through the forest over sandbanks and dead logs. At
the point where they met the rivers widened to form a pool, and here all day
long brilliantly-colored kingfishers flashed up and down between the water and
the surrounding trees. On the far side the bank rose steeply to the plateau of the
reserved forest; magnificent trees over a hundred feet tall, with long branches
interlocking with each other, towered above the river and from there spread in
an even roof to the Nepal border five miles away. Underneath, in an eerie
landscape of bare tree trunks and creepers, was the home of the tiger, the leopard, the sloth bear and many other animals in retreat from man.

It seemed to me then, standing beside the river and listening to the intense
buzz of insects in the forest all around me, that I had found the place I was
looking for. It was as far as I could go in that direction, right on the edge of the

Barasingha stags cluster
at Kanha.

plain, and if civilization was bound to catch up in the end, at least it would take some time.

Billy named his new farm "Tiger Haven," not for the great cats whose pug marks crisscrossed it, but for his brother Jaswant, whose Army nickname was "Tiger." As he began to clear his land, surrounded once again by the wildness where he had always felt most comfortable, a curious thing happened: His old obsession with shooting began to disappear, replaced by a growing interest in the lives and habits of the animals that were fast disappearing around him.

The same thing had happened to his late father. Shortly before he was banished from Balrampur, Jasbir Singh had been sitting up over a leopard kill when not one but four leopards ambled into the clearing—most likely a female and three nearly full-grown cubs—and began feeding and playing so intently that they did not bolt even when he lit up a cigarette. He could not bring himself to fire, and when he came down from the tree he swore he would never shoot anything so beautiful again.

In 1960, Billy and Balram were returning from an evening drive in the forest when they stopped to build a fire and brew a cup of tea. A leopard sawed in the darkness. Billy returned to his jeep, turned on the headlights and edged the vehicle forward. A green pinpoint of light was moving through the trees. He aimed, fired, and the light winked out. When Billy followed it up with a flashlight he found a big leopard lying on the ground. "[A]s I watched, the fire faded from his eyes," he wrote. "I had ... acquired a fine trophy, but I felt nothing but an awful confusion—futility at the destruction of beauty and the taking of life for personal pleasure. I put aside my rifle as my father had done many years before." Soon he was tracking tigers daily with a camera, catching them swimming in the river behind his house or feeding upon the baits he tied for them, becoming more and more obsessed by them.

I asked him once just what it was about tigers that so gripped his imagination. In answering, it seemed to me that Billy was describing not only the qualities he most admired about the tiger but also those he has labored to develop within himself. "The tiger is the symbol of power," he said, "unbridled, elemental. Then of course there's the fact that he's maligned. He's got a finer character than the lion, doesn't quarrel over kills. And he lives alone, unblemished, unmarred. The more you know about him, the more he gets into your imagination."

In any case, having decided he would no longer hunt himself, Billy began to undermine hunting by others. The forest around Billy's new farm formed part of one of forty shooting blocks in Uttar Pradesh which eager *shikaris* and their clients leased by the month. Billy did not want anyone shooting in the forest he now considered his. He leased the block two or three times a year by applying under five or six different names in order to provide his animals temporary sanctuary, and when he could not manage that, he took to waiting till dark, then untying the baits put out by professional *shikaris*.

But it was saving the *barasingha*, or swamp deer—a magnificent, big-antlered animal whose name literally means "twelve-tined"—that became Billy's first conservation cause, and he went about it in characteristically straightforward fashion. Huge herds of barasingha had once lived in Kheri District, so many that an annual shoot was held on the shores of Mirchia Lake during which thousands of animals were driven past the guns of the local ruler and his guests and up to fifty stags were slaughtered in a morning. But it was the post-independence destruction of the swamps and

During the rutting season, barasingha festoon their antlers with grass to overawe rivals.

grasslands in which they had lived for centuries that brought about their precipitous decline.

By the early 1960s, only a single herd of perhaps six hundred animals survived outside the reserve forest, at Ghola, a marshy 3,000-acre plot just eight miles from Tiger Haven. Billy urged the government of Uttar Pradesh to move quickly to take over the tract, add it to the adjacent forest, and declare the whole a permanent reserve before the barasingha were wiped out.

The government dithered. Two years went by. Meanwhile, landless families began crowding onto the grassland. Cattle soon competed with the swamp deer for fodder, and poachers began doing a brisk business peddling deer meat in the Palia bazaar. The herd shrank steadily.

Billy decided he could wait no longer. Before Ghola was overrun by human beings, he would himself lure the deer onto another marshy meadow within the Reserve Forest and adjacent to his farm. He drove his tractor inside the forest, plowed five-acre strips of land, sowed them with barley and established salt licks along the edges. But as soon as the barley began to sprout, cattle devoured it. If Billy's scheme were to succeed, they would have to go. The problem was that they were grazing within the forest legally; their owners had paid an entrance fee for the privilege. "The only effective course of action," Billy wrote later, "was to adopt strong-arm tactics." He caught three graziers who were illegally gathering fallen swamp-deer horns for sale, tied them to his jeep, and paraded them through the forest before turning them over to the Forest Department. The next day they and their cattle were gone.

Billy had readied a new home for the barasingha. Now, he had to persuade them to move into it. Eight miles and the Soheli River separated Ghola from Tiger Haven. To persuade the deer to travel that distance, he borrowed five elephants and their mahouts from a *shikar* outfitter, and—himself in the lead, atop his own elephant—drove the deer before him, firing a shotgun shell into the air to spur them on. Some animals doubled back and disappeared, but at the end of the day more than 450 swamp deer had churned across the Soheli and reached his salt licks and relative safety.

But Billy wasn't through. Graziers returned, their herds consuming precious fodder, and bringing in potential sources of deadly disease. With the help of a sympathetic divisional forest officer, Billy personally lit their cattle camps on fire. Herds and herdsmen ran for their lives. Poachers and timber thieves began creeping into the forest, though Billy did his best to stop them, pummeling with his big fists any who were unfortunate enough to come within reach. And when fishermen slipped in to seine the forest's streams and ponds, he ripped their nets to shreds with his bare hands. The list of his enemies was growing.

Though he did his best to patrol the forest daily, even he knew he could not protect it by himself, and so began a year's tireless lobbying in the state capital of Lucknow to have it declared a wildlife sanctuary. The *shikar* industry opposed Billy bitterly. The Forest Department worried that its commercial exploitation of the forest would be halted. But Billy prevailed, and within five years more than twelve hundred barasingha were flourishing on its broad meadows. In 1964, some 82 square miles of forest were declared as the Dudhwa Wildlife Sanctuary; it had more than doubled in size thirteen years later, thanks to still further lobbying, and became a national park.

The desperate plight of the barasingha had moved Billy to create Dudhwa. But it was the survival of the great cats that preyed upon them that would eventually take over his life and bring him into open confrontation with the Forest Department.

In 1968, the export of wild furs was officially banned over the noisy objections of traders in skins, and there was a growing movement to call a halt to hunting, as well. *Shikar* outfitters launched a counteroffensive: India could not afford to deny itself the precious foreign exchange provided by their foreign clients, they argued; unless their numbers were kept down by shooting, tigers would breed too fast and turn into man-eaters. It seemed likely that the butchery business would go on as usual.

But wildlife had a friend in Prime Minister Indira Gandhi, and when in November 1969 the International Union for the Conservation of Nature held its triennial meeting at New Delhi, she made her feelings clear. "No doubt we need more foreign exchange," Mrs. Gandhi told the assembly, "but not at the cost of the life and liberty of some of the most beautiful species in our country." With the prime minister on their side and the tiger now officially designated as an endangered species, the conservationists' prospects improved overnight. "From being a catch phrase, wildlife became a serious commitment of government," one conservationist remembered. "The ministers got involved; all those who had hindered now began to help."

In 1970, thanks to pressure from Billy and others, India banned all shooting of tigers. Two years later, Parliament passed the Wild Life Protection Act, which barred the killing of sixty more endangered species, provided stiff penalties for those who dared disobey, and laid out the legal framework for enforcement.

And in 1973, backed by a million-dollar pledge from the World Wildlife Fund, the Government of India launched Project Tiger. It had twin objectives—"to ensure the maintenance of a viable population of tigers" and "to preserve for all time, areas of biological importance as a national heritage for the benefit, education and enjoyment of the people." The core areas of the tiger reserves, off-limits to humans, were meant to be "breeding nuclei, from which surplus animals would emigrate to adjacent forests." Broad buffer zones, into which human incursions were to be severely limited, were to shield the breeding grounds from disturbance. Nine existing sanctuaries were designated as tiger reserves. (That number has since grown to nineteen, and there is talk of an eventual total of thirty Project Tiger Reserves.)

Financial responsibility for the reserves was to be divided equally between the states and the central government at New Delhi, but the task of managing them was given over to the Forest Departments of the states alone. Billy and others argued then—and still argue—that this was a grave error: since Indian foresters were trained to manage forests for commercial exploitation, not as safe havens for wildlife, there was from the beginning a built-in conflict of interest. Instead, Project Tiger should either have been the responsibility of the Ministry of Tourism (so that a proportion of the funds spent by visitors to the reserves could be plowed back into them, as in parts of Africa), or placed under a new and entirely separate wildlife organization modeled after the U.S. Fish and Wildlife Service.

To create the reserves, the local populations would be called upon to make great sacrifices: thousands of villagers would have to be moved from their forest homes; the grazing of livestock and gathering of wood and grass and wild honey that had gone on for centuries would abruptly end.

That same spring of 1973 marked the end of the first phase of an experiment that had once more transformed Billy's life. It had begun in 1971, when Anne Wright and her daughter Belinda, old friends from Calcutta, presented him with a three-month-old leopard cub found in Bihar after a party of hunters had killed its mother. He was reluctant to take it at first. He already owned two elephants and over the years had always kept pets—an apparently inexhaustible procession that included dogs and monkeys, goats and chickens, two wolves, a fishing cat, a tiger cub (that died of pneumonia after only a month in Billy's care), and several deer, among them a chital stag that could not be dissuaded from trying to skewer the cook with its antlers. And the three leopards that had prowled around Tiger Haven when he first moved there had all been destroyed by hunters eager for their skins.

But he also knew that raising a leopard would be a grave responsibility. He had farming to do. There were laborers and their families living on his land whose lives might be at risk. He knew nothing of how to raise or feed or train a leopard to survive and prosper on its own; and though he had read with fascination the bestsellers by Joy and George Adamson that detailed how they had returned lions to the wild, he was by no means sure he was equipped to duplicate their feat with a leopard in India.

But once the leopard arrived—more than two feet long, weighing about thirty pounds, insatiably curious, with big floppy paws and a long, twitching tail—he found himself able to think of very little else. Billy named him Prince and introduced him gingerly to his dog, Eelie, a mongrel with a twisted, eel-like tale, who lost no time in asserting her dominance over the cat which, when grown, could easily have made a meal of her.

Two tigers contemplate crossing the Neora River at Dudhwa National Park in Uttar Pradesh.

The leopard's adjustment to life at Tiger Haven was not effortless: in his frenzy to get at his bowl of food, Prince once knocked a friend of Billy's into the Neora, and he routinely bowled over the photographers who came to snap him, delighted in tearing bedding to shreds with his claws, had to be coaxed into entering the jungle where Billy hoped he would one day want to live, took to leaping into the laps of visitors at tea-time in hopes of cadging a piece of buttered toast.

Billy's mother, a frequent visitor to the farm, had always encouraged Billy's love of animals—indeed, he believes he inherited it from her. But she took a distinctly jaundiced view of Prince and the three great cats that came after him, and to relieve her anxiety, Billy had built for her a wire enclosure roofed with thatch and called "Gran's Cage," in which she contentedly spent her days, knitting, playing solitaire, or entertaining guests while her son's big pets prowled outside. The arrangement startled some visitors; but to Billy, a world in which the people were caged and the animals allowed to roam free now increasingly seemed the natural order of things.

Then two incidents occurred which persuaded Billy that there would have to be serious changes at Tiger Haven. Twice, Prince leaped upon small girls, claws bared. Neither was seriously mauled—Billy believes that to a leopard, small children, with their thin limbs and rapid movements, seem not to be human beings but some form of monkey, and monkeys are a staple in their diet—but something clearly had to be done.

Billy insisted that his servants send their children home to their villages to remove temptation. For all intents and purposes, he abandoned farming for profit, relying instead on donations from people interested in his work with wild animals and the handful of tourists who could be lured to the *terai* to stay with him, and raising only crops that would benefit the deer and jungle fowl that slipped into his fields morning and evening. Now, local people, already bewildered by the powerful, taciturn man who lived alone and patrolled the forest behind his house like an avenging demon, became convinced that he was half-mad, preferring the company of a dangerous leopard to that of other human beings.

Billy paid no attention. Determined to get Prince to move into the forest and away from the farm, he built him a forest treehouse about a mile from Tiger Haven. At first, the leopard was happy enough to climb up to it but, for fear of the tigers whose territory surrounded it, refused to climb back down again unless Billy were waiting at the ladder's foot with his bowl of food.

Then disaster struck. While Billy was away on a visit to Delhi, the man who took care of one of his elephants brought his eight-year-old son to the farm. The leopard wandered past the building in which they lived and either out of fright or playfulness, the boy poked at him with a stick. Prince seized him by the head, bit deep, and held on as the boy screamed in terror. His father leaped up and managed to pry open the leopard's jaws, but his son's skull was fractured.

The victim was rushed first to one hospital, then another. He seemed to be improving, but developed sepsis and eventually died.

The District Magistrate ordered Billy either to cage Prince and send him to a zoo or to have him destroyed. Billy built a sturdy cage—if Prince were to be incarcerated, it would be on his farm—then, desperate to see his experiment through, he invited the Forest Secretary of Uttar Pradesh, who happened to be in the neighborhood, and several other officials to come to Tiger Haven and see for themselves whether or not Prince was a menace.

In the end, some fifty nervous visitors piled out of a dozen vehicles to inspect the leopard. Prince behaved "impeccably," Billy remembered, rubbing himself against his visitors' legs, allowing himself to be scratched, jumping from the hood of one car to the next.

The Forest Secretary was convinced that the attack on the boy, tragic as it was, had been provoked, an aberration. The leopard was declared state property and Billy's experiment an official project. A sign reading "LEOPARD PROJECT" went up at the end of the dirt track that leads to Tiger Haven; it forbade women and children from visiting the farm except in closed cars.

Billy returned to his work. It took months of effort, but Prince began clumsily to kill on his own, small game at first (peacocks, rhesus monkeys, a porcupine) and then several chital whose carcasses Billy had to open at first so the leopard could eat. By the time Prince was twenty months old and nearly full grown, he was spending more and more time on his own.

Late in the afternoon of May 24, 1973, Billy left his house with his camera, hoping to photograph a tiger whose movements he'd been following. Suddenly, Prince emerged from the trees on the opposite side of the Neora, stalked out onto a projecting log and settled down for nearly half an hour, staring at the farm on which he had been raised. Then he rose to his feet, called twice and melted into the forest.

Billy never saw him again; "wherever he had gone," he wrote, "he had triumphantly vindicated my experiment in rehabilitation."

He was not alone for long; within a few weeks of Prince's departure, Prime Minister Indira Gandhi had presented him with two female leopard cubs. Billy named them Harriet and Juliette after English friends, and kept them close to home in the hope that when grown, one or the other of them might lure Prince back to the forest behind Tiger Haven, and away from the unprotected Nepal border toward which he had wandered and where Billy feared he was likely to be shot.

The mid-seventies were the worst and the best of years for Billy. First, Juliette was

At Tiger Haven, on the edge of Dudhwa, Tara makes it clear to Billy Arjan Singh that she'd really rather not have her picture taken.

found dead in the Neora shallows, evidently poisoned by someone convinced that Billy's leopards were responsible for the deaths of domestic livestock actually taken by an abandoned sub-adult tiger. Billy was devastated: Juliette had been the gentlest and most affectionate of his leopards. "The memory of her soft little grunts of welcome, now still forever, made me feel unashamedly as though I had lost a child," he wrote later. "For a man to sacrifice an animal whose species has already suffered so much from human persecution and greed, was an act which I hope will be answerable on the Day of Judgment."

Then, instead of trying to capture the errant tiger cub, as required by statute, a park official summarily shot it. It turned out to weigh just fifty pounds. Billy was enraged: "When I pointed out that a million dollars had been subscribed all over the world to ensure the tiger's safety, and insisted that action was needed to prevent the animal being destroyed by little men in authority who ignored what the law explicitly stated, an atmosphere of hatred quickly built up."

That atmosphere would continue to build and has never really abated. In August 1975, monsoon waters drowned much of the forest, driving Harriet back to Tiger Haven to find shelter. Before Billy was unavoidably called away to Delhi, he repeated his long-standing order that no children be brought to Tiger Haven, and as a further precaution added that his watchman, Gajbir, who was to sleep inside one of the buildings, must keep his door locked.

But as soon as Billy left, Gajbir brought his twelve-year-old son, Sikandar, to stay the night with him, then left the door ajar to catch whatever wisp of breeze might stir the sodden air. Sometime during the night, Harriet slipped inside the room, saw both figures sleeping on the floor, and, perhaps confused, as Prince once had been, by a child's resemblance to a langur, seized him by the throat. Sikandar bled to death.

"THE ANIMALS HAVE FIRST PRECEDENCE HERE" reads a sign today inside the main Dudhwa gate; at Tiger Haven that is literally true. Billy's reaction to the tragedy was, first, fury at the hapless father who had disobeyed his orders; then anxiety for fear

Tara and Billy.

the normally docile character of his leopard had somehow been permanently altered.

With his tracker, Babu Lal, he got into his flat-bottomed rowboat and started upriver to find Harriet:

> ... I called repeatedly, but she neither appeared nor answered, and I had just decided to go back when Babu Lal suddenly cried, "Here she comes!"
> I looked up to see her running down the slope. She hopped into the boat and absolutely overwhelmed me with affection. First she rubbed herself against me like a huge domestic cat; then she put her paws on my shoulders and started grooming my head. As her rough tongue rasped over my hair, I felt my eyes fill with tears of pleasure and relief. She had not changed in the slightest. ... Her ancestry and instincts had equipped her to do precisely what she had done when she had found the boy on the floor. We humans should have prevented the situation arising.

Prince did return to Tiger Haven to mate with Harriet—at least Billy believes it was Prince—and she bore two cubs, which she carried home to the second floor of Tiger Haven during the rains. But both died within three months: the first killed and eaten by a tigress; the second drowned when Harriet tried to swim with it across the swollen Neora.

A less determined man would have given up after such disappointments. Prince had apparently been successfully reintroduced into the jungle, though at the cost of one child's life. But Juliette had been poisoned, while Harriet had killed a second child and could not be said ever to have become truly wild, since she continued to spend much of her time in the company of humans at Tiger Haven. Meanwhile, rumors continued to circulate through the fearful countryside about the strange man who lived with leopards.

Billy would not be discouraged. In fact, he had still another more controversial reintroduction scheme in mind. With the tigers' numbers alarmingly low and no guarantee that Project Tiger would be able to increase them, he was determined to demonstrate that tigers, too, could be returned to the jungle.

He persuaded Mrs. Gandhi to give the project her official sanction. A three-month-old female cub named Jane was found at the Twycross Zoo in England, and Billy flew there to pick her up. He renamed her Tara, and had just succeeded in winning her over—after suffering a number of bites and scratches and sacrificing a pair of good trousers to her claws—when a wildlife official called from Delhi, urging Billy to abandon his latest scheme: Tara's lineage included a remote Siberian ancestor; she should not be released in India for fear she would transfer genetic impurities to the Indian species. Billy angrily ignored the call. "It struck me as a most ludicrous scientific quibble," he wrote later, "when every effort was being made to save the tiger from extinction." It was an early skirmish in a long and increasingly acrimonious war.

Billy brought Tara back to Tiger Haven and introduced her to Harriet and to his dog Eelie—who nipped the big newcomer's flank in order to assert her dominance, just as she had with all three leopards. Harriet had lost one of her cubs to a tigress and was understandably slower to adjust, but before long the three animals and Billy became inseparable.

Film footage of life at Tiger Haven in those days, made by a British film crew, is irresistible: Tara bounds onto her protector's back, biting fondly at his head and neck until the small but authoritative dog knocks the tigress off her beaming master; in the heart of the forest, flanked by giant sal trees lit with Wagnerian shafts of sunlight, Billy strolls down the road, while behind him pad the dog, the tigress, and the leopard, their tails twitching in unlikely unison; Eelie bounds after Harriet and Tara as they dash into the forest, then race back to rub their sides against Billy's thick legs; Tara, her ears just visible above the yellow grass that perfectly masks her coat, watches inscrutably as a herd of uneasy barasingha edges deeper into the forest.

Tara stayed with Billy for about two years, remaining affectionate and playful all the while, but, since she eventually weighed nearly three hundred pounds, her high-spirited leaps onto Billy's back and their boat trips across the river together could be hazardous. She managed to kill a peacock (though Billy had to pluck it for her before she would make a meal of it), a porcupine, a sambar fawn, and she slowly began to spend more and more time on her own in the forest.

Two male tigers separately began to visit the farm toward the end of 1977, evidently drawn by her presence, and on January 16 of the following year, she vanished with one of them into the Dudhwa forest.

By the end of 1978 Billy would find himself alone again, with only Eelie to provide him with the animal companionship he craved. Harriet had successfully mated for a second time and given birth to a single female cub, delivered in an upstairs bathroom during the preceding monsoon, but she had unaccountably abandoned it early, and in June it was killed by a train. A few months later, Harriet herself was found dead, perhaps poisoned by people frightened she would take another human life. "Her death was a shattering blow to me.... For many weeks I could not speak about her without being overcome by emotion ... I felt I had lost a daughter."

Without the company of a great cat, Billy would never again be entirely happy.

CHAPTER FIVE

# NO AX FALLS

After Project Tiger's first two years, its first director, a veteran Rajasthan forest officer named Kailash Sankhala, published a book in which he included a euphoric progress report:

In India we who manage the reserves are all foresters. In forestry we are used to the slow growth of trees and do not expect to enjoy the fruits of our labor in our lifetime. But the success of Project Tiger in just two years has dazzled even the field directors. No ax falls on any tree, no saw moves on dead or fallen wood....

The springs have revived. The flowers bloom, no longer browsed by domestic stock. The ungulates have all the space they need and their population has increased. Tiger sightings are more frequent and there has been a baby boom....

The project has fully demonstrated that by tradition and training the Indian forester is much better equipped to administer a conservation project than anyone else....

Things were never so rosy as that, but Sankhala's initial enthusiasm was understandable. Although by the time I began visiting Indian National Parks and Project Tiger reserves in the mid-1980s there were already disquieting rumors that all was not as it seemed, the sights and sounds I experienced were unforgettable.

Driving through the jungles of the Central Indian state of Madhya Pradesh for the first time, I had the eerie feeling that I already knew the hills and ravines, forests and villages through which we were passing. In a sense I did, for Madhya Pradesh forms part of the old Central Provinces, and it was here that Mowgli, the hero of Rudyard Kipling's *Jungle Books,* was supposed to have lived out his adventures.

My grandmother first read the Mowgli stories to me when I was a very small boy, her patient voice punctuated by the click of her knitting needles, and, later, when I encountered Tarzan on my own, he seemed in every sense a pale imitation. Kipling's vivid characters remained with me forty-odd years later—Mowgli, the brash village boy raised by wolves; Baloo, the world-weary old bear that tried to teach him the Law of the Jungle; Kaa, the great gray python that grew fond of Mowgli; Sher Khan, the tiger that wished only to eat him.

Kipling himself never actually saw the jungles he described—he spent most of his time in India in the Punjab, far to the north, and wrote the *Jungle Books* in Vermont—but for anyone steeped in his Mowgli stories, a visit to Kanha and Bandhavgarh national parks in Madhya Pradesh nonetheless seemed something like a homecoming.

In Mowgli's time, the whole region was canopied with trees and the number of wild animals living in their shade was prodigious. In 1923, a British forest officer fondly recalled how it had been in a single shooting block when he was young: "In

*Opposite:* A tigress and two nineteen-month-old cubs dabble undisturbed in a pool in the heart of Ranthambhore.

1900, this tract contained as much game as any tract I ever saw in the best parts of Africa.... I have seen 1500 head consisting of eleven species in an evening's stroll. It is nothing like that now, but it is probably true to say that it contains more numbers and species than any other tract of its size in the whole of Asia."

He was writing of the grassy meadows that now form the heart of Kanha National Park. Kanha is one of the largest national parks in India—nearly 2,000 square kilometers—and for many years was in the charge of one of Project Tiger's ablest field directors, H. S. Panwar.

Indian wildlife is as rich and varied as any on earth, but it ordinarily cannot be viewed as easily as can, say, that of the East African plains. For the most part, Indian birds and animals flourish in thick forest or dense scrub jungle and must be sought out, not simply stared at. But driving slowly through the Kanha meadows—grassy clearings left behind when a series of villages were shifted out more than a century ago—I saw hundreds of deer, including scores of the hard-ground barasingha, a variant of the animal Billy struggled to save at Dudhwa that survives only here. It was the rutting season and the stags strutted through the tall grass, their great spreading horns festooned with branches to intimidate their rivals. Fawns gamboled about the edges of the herd, tails twitching, ears barely visible above the foliage.

During the long drives we took each morning and evening, I saw other sights impossible to forget: A herd of seven gaur, the largest hoofed animal in Asia, six feet at the shoulder, and so massive and so powerful that they seem like buffalo on steroids, pushing their way through the trees and the early morning mist just twenty feet from our Land Rover; two tiny four-horned antelope scurrying off through the undergrowth, followed by their still more diminutive offspring, no larger than a house-cat; a sounder of sixteen wild boar jumping, one by one, across the road ahead of us, silhouetted against the setting sun like so many targets in a shooting gallery.

But it was a *sound* I heard at Kanha that remains with me most vividly.

Late one afternoon we parked on the edge of the largest meadow. Everything seemed idyllic. Half a dozen chital browsed beneath a clump of trees. Silver-gray langur monkeys played in the branches above them. The distant clatter of two far-off barasingha stags locking horns drifted toward us. A cool breeze feathered the tall grass.

Suddenly, the spotted deer froze, ears up. One frantic doe barked in terror, her left front hoof held high, then leaped into the air and skipped sideways fifteen yards. The monkeys danced up and down with rage.

The doe had spotted a tiger, invisible to us, and just made it out of harm's way.

The tiger roared. The sound seemed to split the air. It was the loudest, angriest noise I've ever heard, and he repeated it five times. His frustration was understandable: a big tiger devours upward of sixty pounds of meat a night, and the American field biologist George B. Schaller, who based his classic study *The Deer and the Tiger* on observations made at Kanha in the early 1960s, found that on the average Kanha tigers made at least twenty tries before managing to kill.

The meadow in front of us fell quiet again. The deer returned to their ceaseless munching; the monkeys groomed one another's fur. After three minutes or so, faint alarm calls reached us from the distant tree line. Another deer had spotted the hungry tiger as he moved on.

The tiger ruled here, just as Sher Khan did in Mowgli's jungle, and the whole forest vibrated to his movements.

Kipling came to mind again as we left Kanha for Bandhavgarh National Park, not part of the Project Tiger network but celebrated for its tigers nonetheless. We passed over the tumbling Wainganga River, beneath whose turbulent surface Mowgli hid from a hive of angry bees, and along the edge of the Seeonee Hills, where his wolfpack had its den; the Indian wolf has been all but obliterated from Central India since, and the rocky hills themselves have been largely stripped of jungle by villagers seeking firewood.

Like many Indian national parks, Bandhavgarh was originally the exclusive hunting preserve of a princely family. The Maharajas of Rewa, best known to zoo-goers for the white tigers bred in another nearby sanctuary, were then its exclusive beneficiaries, and dinner at the Bandhavgarh Jungle Camp where we stayed was still being served each evening in the big, gloomy dining room of their old hunting lodge, its tall, pale green walls forested with antlers. His last Highness was an inveterate killer of tigers as well as deer, and a handsome stone monument marks the spot just a few miles down the road on which he chalked up his hundredth; she turned out to be a fairly unimpressive young tigress, but could still be seen—stuffed, labeled, and only slightly the worse for wear—in the parlor of the lodge.

A trained naturalist was in charge, Hashim Tyabji, an enthusiastic, bespectacled young Indian from a distinguished Muslim family. There seemed little he didn't know about the jungle and its inhabitants, and he was willing to impart as much or as little of it as his visitors liked as he escorted them through the park.

We started off at dawn each morning with Hashim at the wheel of the jeep. At the gate, a blue and black signboard offered an exhortation of the kind of which Indian Forest departments seem universally fond: "MATCHLESS BEAUTY OF BANDHAVGARH NATIONAL PARK INSPIRES US TO LOVE THE NATURE. PLEASE ABIDE BY THE RULES TO AVOID DISCOMFORT."

I asked Hashim just what kind of discomfort he thought might result from rule breaking. "They don't want you to walk," he said. "Tigers."

Very sensible, it seemed to me. Bandhavgarh was said to be unusually rich in tigers.

This park is much smaller than Kanha—though it has recently more than doubled

Hashim Tyabji in the hilltop fort at Bandhavgarh.

its size, to 450 square kilometers—and it lacks the larger park's spectacular meadows, but it encompasses a whole range of wooded hills and a handsome hilltop fortress.

As he drove, Hashim seemed to miss nothing, pointing out birds and animals where I could have sworn nothing breathed: A crested serpent eagle sitting motionless in the top of a tree just inside the gate, regal and withdrawn; a few yards further on, a minute collared Scops owl glowering out of its hole in the hollow trunk of the tree against which it was all but invisible.

Once, he wrenched the jeep off the road into an abandoned field and we rattled slowly toward what I was sure was simply a reddish clod of earth. It turned out to be a sleeping fox. We parked no more than fifty feet away while it woke up and went through a brisk repertoire of foxy poses—yawning, stretching, scratching, snapping up a passing locust, dozing off again.

Between visitors, Hashim spent as much time in the jungle as he could on his own, mapping the territories of the tigers nearest to camp, and making meticulous notes on all that he saw and heard in a tiny spiral notebook.

He had also taken it upon himself to conduct the park's first systematic bird census, and had already identified 213 species when we visited him and was still eagerly adding to his tally every day. At least forty-four different kinds of birds flapped and cawed and whirred in and out of the trees that shaded the campsite itself, and their names only hinted at their exotic variety—green barbets, golden orioles, blossom-headed parakeets, blue-bearded bee-eaters, and a big hornbill, whose head looked so top-heavy that flying itself seemed a miracle.

We backed up and left the fox, and soon stopped again, this time at the edge of a shallow pond, its edges fringed with reeds, to watch the waterbirds. A black-bellied tern angrily stabbed the still surface again and again without pinning its prey.

"Beautiful bird. Bad fisherman," Hashim muttered.

Nearby, a turquoise common kingfisher had better luck: it hovered for what seemed a full minute above a mirror image of itself, then plunged and came up with a furiously wriggling silver fish.

"Well done, old chap," Hashim said, and we moved on. The real law of the jungle is distinctly unsentimental.

The soft, dusty surface of the roads that snake through the forest records much of the life that takes place along it, and as we drove along Hashim explained what some of the clues meant. Those tiny, delicate claw marks were left by a gray mongoose—Rikki-Tikki-Tavi thrives at Bandhavgarh, though he is largely nocturnal and therefore hard to see. The big splayed tracks of a peacock traced concentric circles across the road, evidence that he had danced here, whirling and frantically waving his great tail in hopes of seducing one or another of his perpetually preoccupied hens. A meandering line of big, five-toed, oddly humanoid footprints led to a deep crater in the center of the road; it had been newly dug, Hashim explained as he swung wide to avoid our falling in, by a sloth bear in search of juicy termites. (Baloo, Mowgli's shaggy, avuncular tutor, was a Himalayan brown bear, a species which in real life has always been foreign to these parts; as a naturalist, Kipling turns out to have been a fine short story writer.)

We followed the fresh pug marks of a big tiger that had padded along the road on his nightly patrol for nearly two kilometers. A tree leaned in from the right and Hashim stopped the jeep, jumped down and sniffed its bark; the tiger had sprayed it

*Opposite:* Gaur emerge from the trees to graze in a meadow at Bandhavgarh.

during the night to mark his territory. I got down, too. The residue has a not unpleasant, musky smell, very different from the cat-box reek I'd expected.

We saw no tiger from the jeep, and so at dawn one morning we joined the little fleet of three park elephants that sets out daily in search of tigers to show to visitors. It was still dark and cold when we clambered onto our mount and lumbered off. We took the lead; four other visitors rode each of the others.

Our mahout wore woolen toe socks to keep warm as he performed the gentle but relentless tap dance behind his elephant's ears that guided her along the proper path, and a walkie-talkie was stuffed into his jacket pocket so that he could report back to park headquarters every few minutes on what he had found; its intermittent staticky crackle was unnerving in the otherwise silent forest. Still, Mowgli would have felt himself on familiar ground.

A tigress with two half-grown cubs had been seen killing a spotted deer high on the slope the previous evening, and so, after plodding our way across the valley floor through dewy grass twice as high as an elephant's eye, we started up the steep hillside. As she climbed, our mount placed each barrel-sized foot with ponderous delicacy. The *idea* of elephant-riding is alarming, the reality reassuring; the thing to do is enjoy the marvelous view from twelve feet off the ground, roll with the steady sway rather than fight it, and keep in mind that—unlike, say, a jeep—this vehicle thinks for herself and has at least as large a stake in staying upright as have her passengers.

It took us more than an hour to find the tigress, a sudden, vivid orange against the forest floor and, as always, far larger than I'd imagined. She lay out in the open alongside her half-eaten kill, and seemed utterly unconcerned as three elephants crashed to within thirty feet of her and stopped while our mahout reported in to his superiors on the walkie-talkie and the excited riders talked to one another, changed lenses, discussed focal lengths, and passed cameras back and forth between the elephants.

Nothing we mere humans did seemed to faze her. She soon fell noisily asleep, belly up, one huge hind paw in the air. Not even the faint mewing of her hungry cubs, hidden somewhere further up the hillside, interrupted her. We watched for half an hour or so. One eye did open when the shadow of a low-flying vulture passed over her, but her only real sign of annoyance during all that time was a sudden, hissing snarl when a gray tree-pie, hopping across the ground, ventured too close to her kill. Hashim whispered: "Tigers do not like to *share*."

The story I remember best from the *Jungle Books* was "Kaa's Hunting," in which a troop of gray, long-tailed langur monkeys kidnap Mowgli and carry him off to the abandoned, overgrown city they call the Cold Lairs.

Kipling's langurs are perfectly evoked:

Here we sit in a branchy row,
Thinking of beautiful things we know.
Dreaming of deeds that we mean to do,
All complete, in a minute or two—
Something noble and wise and good,
Done by merely wishing we could.
We've forgotten, but—never mind
*Brother, thy tail hangs down behind!*

For all their silvery grace and the deceptive gravity of their wizened black faces,

A tigress and her cubs at Kanha.

langurs do seem constitutionally unable to concentrate for very long on any one task. A tribe of perhaps twenty bounded into camp one afternoon, hooting as they crashed from tree to tree; some used the taut roofs of the tents as trampolines, others stuffed their mouths with berries, two poked their heads into our tent, evidently on the lookout for the bright, shiny shampoo bottles Hashim said they especially enjoyed stealing.

A boy with a catapult followed them across the floor of the clearing, hurling stones up into the branches to drive them off. They dodged the missiles, chattered down at their tormentor and showered him with leaves and branches, then left, as loudly and apparently pointlessly as they had come.

The picturesque ruin Kipling actually had in mind when he conjured up the monkeys' ghost city of Cold Lairs was the citadel of Amber, high above Jaipur, the capital of far-off Rajasthan; it was indeed eerie and deserted when Kipling visited it in 1887, but Mowgli would no longer recognize it for the busloads of eager tourists who now push through its corridors and overflow its courtyards.

He would still feel right at home at Bandhavgarh.

On the broad top of the highest hill within the park—a 580-acre plateau flattened, according to local legend, by the angry stamping of the god Rama, and thickly overgrown with grass and trees and vines—lie the crumbling remains of a thousand-year-old fortress. The plateau was still the property of the Rewa royal family and off-limits to park visitors unwilling to make the steep climb on foot, but the proprietors of the camp had the exclusive right to clank their way up the slope by jeep.

On our last morning in camp we made that trip, whining uphill past elaborate caves chiseled into the hillside so long ago that their purpose is no longer known.

After a savage tug-of-war with crocodiles lurking in the lake, a tigress and her eager cubs lay claim to a sambar kill at Ranthambhore.

Near the top, a lofty gateway and massive wooden doors studded with brass spikes barred our way. A servant jumped down with a big brass key, unlocked the great doors and eased them open.

At least one tiger included this hilltop within his territory, for it is the home of several varieties of deer and a small herd of black buck, descendants of a pair released here some years ago by the Maharaja. As our jeep nosed through the undergrowth, a big male antelope bounded away, leaping effortlessly above the tall grass, his long twisting horns tucked back along his neck. In fact, the jungle is so thick that it is hard at first to make out the remnants of the city that once stood here. But Hashim began to point out the ruins—deep, rock-cut tanks still filled with green water, tumbled walls that marked a palace, schools, barracks, an armory and a treasure house, and a series of intricately carved temples, each dedicated to one of the nine main *avatars*, or incarnations, of Vishnu—eagle, tortoise, fish, and wild boar among them.

The sole human resident of the ancient fortress was an elderly priest who still officiated at the largest shrine. He was a tall, sober man with a huge, deep voice, understandably eager to see visitors and to demonstrate his command of half a dozen English words. After offering us a bit of *prasad*—a dingy wedge of coconut blessed by having been in the presence of the sacred images—the pandit led us down a steep path to see several other temples. Broken gods and goddesses lay everywhere along the slope, and when we took too much time exclaiming over them, the old man grew impatient and strode on ahead. This was his hill, clearly; these were his deities; and he was determined to set the pace.

When we caught up with him, he was standing before a small shrine, pointing a long finger inside. We bent and peered into the darkness: the interior was almost entirely filled with a huge fish, hewn from a single block of stone; its goggle eyes and round mouth bore faint traces of orange daub, indicating that it had been venerated fairly recently.

"Some fish!" I said to Diane.

The old priest drew himself up, pleased that we were pleased, and proudly shouted what he was sure was its English name: "WILD BOAR!"

We drove to the other side of the hilltop, scattering clouds of tiny quail. Two painted partridges drummed away into the grass as we parked at the plateau's edge. A fire was built and breakfast was prepared—fried eggs, toast and jam, fresh tea—while we sprawled on rocks and gazed down upon the park.

Just twenty feet or so below us, a griffon vulture glided above the rocky slope into which its nest was tucked. Looking down on it as it rode the streams and eddies of the air, I could clearly hear the wind whistling through its widespread wings. Below the big, suspended bird, the green valleys and blue, forested hills stretched away in all directions, teeming with life just as they had in Mowgli's time.

Corbett National Park, located in the Himalayan foothills 180 miles northeast of Delhi, has always been a favorite with foreign visitors. When I first visited it in the winter of 1985, though, they were restricted to a crowded tourist complex called Dikhala in the heart of the forest, and while confined there were forced to eat watery vegetarian fare served from what must surely have been one of the worst kitchens in India while subject to a truly distinctive menace—a wild elephant that seemed to take special pleasure in roaming the parking lot at night, gravely caving in the roof of one car after another by sitting on it.

It is in large part Corbett's terrain that draws the tourists: despite the metaled roads that run through it, and the hortatory slogans painted here and there in bright orange on the stony hillsides—TAKE ONLY PICTURES/LEAVE ONLY FOOTPRINTS—the park still looks much as it must have looked when Jim Corbett was lobbying to have it declared India's first National Park. Its wooded hills and broad grasslands are cut by clear mountain streams and alive with birds and animals. And, despite the cars streaming to and from Dikhala and the noisy families lurching through the grass on elephant-back, it remained genuinely wild.

About eleven-thirty in the morning of February 22, 1985, a British ornithologist named David Hunt was leading a party of eighteen birdwatchers along a dusty path in the heart of the park. Forest guard Harrak Singh walked with him, armed with an old shotgun loaded with buckshot and intended only to be fired into the air to discourage wild elephants from venturing too close.

Hunt had visited the park several times before and knew that no one was ever allowed to leave the paths for any reason. But when he spotted a large and unusual owl sitting in a tree high on a slope, he and two friends decided they would climb up to see if they could get a picture. Harrak Singh's warnings were ignored.

The climb proved steep and rocky, complicated by thick tangles of lantana and bamboo. When the owl left its perch and flapped further up the hillside, Hunt split off from his companions to try to find an easier route. His friends grew discouraged and returned to the path.

They heard a scream, then silence. Harrak Singh forced his way up the slope, shotgun in hand, until he reached the lip of a natural shelf and cautiously peered over it. The grass in front of him was smeared with dark blood. Hunt's binoculars lay nearby, their strap broken. Further back was Hunt's sprawled body, and beyond it, melting into the forest, was the striped form of a tiger. Harrak Singh hurried down the slope to summon help.

It took several hours for a party to assemble, and another twenty minutes or so to prod eight nervous elephants, each bearing an armed forest guard, into making their ponderous way up the steep slope. By then, the body had been carefully hidden by the tiger in a clump of bamboo.

The great cat was still nearby, some thirty yards up the hillside, pacing back and forth and snarling. Eight shots were fired into the air. The animal would not be scared off. Finally, the elephants were drawn up into a line between the tiger and the bamboo so that the body could be recovered. Hunt's neck had been broken; his left kneecap had been removed as if by a surgeon, and a small portion of his calf appeared to have been eaten.

In the excitement, no one got a very clear description of the tiger, although one member of the party did manage to snap several blurry photographs of it.

Asok Singh, the park's field director, was now faced with a difficult decision. Would the killer strike again? Was this a painful but isolated incident, a tragic accident caused by human heedlessness? Or was it the beginning of a deliberate career of man-eating?

The killing had taken place within the staked-out territory of a male tiger the forest guards called Dhitu, whose disdain for visitors was legend among park personnel.

*Pages 100–101:* Visitors in search of a tiger at Corbett.

A tiger cub less than twenty days old, carefully hidden within the Ranthambhore thicket in which it was born.

He was an immense, glossy animal, weighing perhaps five hundred pounds. He was so impressive and so utterly unconcerned in the presence of humans that he had become a sort of unofficial park mascot, featured on posters and T-shirts. His huge, fresh pug marks were found in a riverbed not far from the hillside up which David Hunt had scrambled to his death. All the available evidence seemed to indicate that Dhitu's lifelong disdain for people had finally turned him into a killer. Reluctantly, the field director announced that the celebrated tiger should be shot.

Five days later, Brijendra Singh arrived. He is a short, sturdy outdoorsman, a member of the same Kapurthala royal family from which Billy Arjan Singh comes and, like his distant cousin, he was once a keen hunter and has become a dedicated conservationist. He lives in a fashionable section of New Delhi, where he quietly and effectively lobbies behind the scenes on behalf of India's wildlife, but he spends as much time as he can each year among Corbett Park's tigers, and he took with great seriousness his status as honorary wildlife warden. Almost exactly one year earlier, he had helped trap a tiger responsible for the death of one elephant handler and the mauling of a second; the animal had been shipped to the Lucknow Zoo, where it subsequently died.

Dhitu was a special favorite of his, and before the tiger was executed he wanted to be certain of its guilt beyond a reasonable doubt.

Brijendra visited the site. The ornithologist's binoculars still lay where they had fallen from his neck at the cliff's edge. A trail of other belongings—a book of matches, Hunt's watch, several crumpled sheets of tissue—marked the trail up which he had been dragged. There was still dried blood beneath the bamboo.

That night, Brijendra had a buffalo calf tied at the base of the hill. It was gone by morning, killed and hauled up the thickly grown slope. He followed the trail until he found the dead buffalo precisely where Hunt's body had been hidden. Clearly, the same tiger had hidden both kills, but there was no tiger to be seen.

Brijendra climbed into a tree with his camera. More than three hours passed.

Once he heard what sounded like the thin yowling of tiger cubs from somewhere further up the slope. Then a striped animal appeared on the hillside above the kill. Not Dhitu, but a young tigress, her belly still loose from having recently given birth to a litter.

Brijendra raised his camera and took several pictures. Later, they would prove a perfect match with those of the animal that the shotguns of the forest guards had failed to intimidate. Her apparent fearlessness was now explained: She had been unwilling to abandon her hidden cubs.

It was now possible to reconstruct exactly what had happened on the hillside six days earlier. On that morning, the tiger had left her cubs safely secreted among the rocks higher up the slope. She had stretched out in the cool grass near the cliff's edge and there had fallen asleep. David Hunt, his eyes on the elusive owl above him, had loomed suddenly over her. Startled, frightened, she had lashed out.

Instinct made her kill. Then it made her hide what she had killed. Finally, it had made her sample that kill. But she had *only* sampled it, and there was no reason she would ever repeat any part of what had now clearly been an inadvertent tragedy.

A few days after David Hunt was killed, Diane and I had a chance to see the exonerated Dhitu. We found him in a pool, up to his chin in the dark, stained water. Our elephant shook with fear as we approached, producing her own low, uneasy rumble. Though we stopped and stood less than thirty feet away from him for at least ten minutes, the tiger paid no attention to us.

After a time he hauled himself out of the water and rolled onto his back, lazily examined one enormous paw, and scratched his wet shoulders on the leafy forest floor. Then he stood up and, gazing intently at us for the first time, sprayed as if to mark as his own the clearing into which we had intruded—emitting a thin, astonishingly forceful stream that flew backwards six or seven feet before hitting the ground. Finally, he lowered his big head and swung off into the trees, going about his business.

That business did eventually come to include killing men. Late in the afternoon of November 29, 1985, a Nepalese laborer named Khan Bahadur was gathering firewood just a few yards from the Khinanoli Rest House, in the heart of the forest. As

Brijendra Singh on elephant-back at Corbett, in search of a man-eater.

Ullas Karanth (*left*), listening for the tell-tale sounds of one of his radio-collared tigers; and K. M. Chinnappa, the range officer responsible for safeguarding the extraordinary richness of Nagarahole National Park in Tamil Nadu.

Bahadur bent over, his arms already full of sticks, to retrieve one more, a tiger struck him from behind. He was dead before his load had clattered to the ground. The tiger dragged him into the undergrowth.

This time, Dhitu clearly was the culprit. His big, unmistakable pug marks—and only his—were found at the scene, and when the park director led a flotilla of ten elephants into the undergrowth a couple of hours after the attack, they found him crouching over the corpse, calmly eating. The tiger was as apparently contemptuous of human beings as ever; nothing Asok Singh and his men could think to do would drive him off his kill. Finally, he worked up enough of a thirst to go for water on his own, allowing the forest guards on elephants time to surround and recover what was left of the body.

Four days later, Brijendra trapped the tiger in a steel cage. Dhitu was dispatched to the zoo at Kanpur, where his reluctant captor visited him. The tiger sired two cubs while in captivity and seemed "quite happy," Brijendra told me, "getting lots of meat."

Perhaps the closest I ever came to glimpsing the wild India turn-of-the-century visitors saw was an afternoon spent sitting in the watchtower that overlooks a water hole in the heart of Nagarahole National Park in the southern state of Karnataka.

Four broad firelines had been cut through the gray-green jungle, and waiting there while the late afternoon shadows lengthened was something like attending an infinitely complex tennis match, my head swiveling back and forth from clearing to clearing as one by one the animals emerged for their evening drink. Each species had its own way of approaching the water. Sambar and chital clung to the tree line, ears twitching with anxiety. Barking deer, red-brown and little larger than cocker spaniels, undulated through the grass, heads down, as if moving through waves. Three wild boar raced for the water, snorting as they went and scaring a pair of peahens into noisy flight.

The larger animals came, too. A young bull elephant splashed into the water, drank his fill, somehow sensed my presence, whirled round and round in melodramatic fury, flapping his ears and trumpeting all the while, then crashed off through the brush.

After things calmed down again, a bull gaur materialized at the water's edge, his body a dark, daunting wall of muscle out of all proportion to his small head and tiny, stockinged feet. Mynah birds flitted on and off his broad back as he lowered his horns to drink.

I spent that evening with Ullas Karanth, an American-trained researcher then setting out on a study of the relationship between prey and predator within the park based on the radio-collaring of tigers and leopards—a technique successfully employed by Smithsonian researchers in Nepal but still new and controversial in India (where, I was told, a Member of Parliament once warned that if permitted in India, the collars would be used by the CIA to transmit secrets back and forth over the Himalayas).

"Ninety-six percent of this country is earmarked for people," Karanth told me. "Only four percent for parks and animals. On that four percent there must be no compromise. We must learn to live with the fact that the park's neighbors will always be hostile. It is primarily a policing job. We can do it if we're serious. You must take a long view. When I first came here in the late 1960s, there was poaching everywhere. Poached tigers were paraded on the road and nobody did anything. Now, there is none of that."

There was none of it at Nagarahole largely because of the unusually dedicated range officer in charge, K. M. Chinnappa. Tall and whippet-thin, with bright, flashing eyes, he had devoted most of his adult life to the welfare of his park. He never wanted to live anywhere else—he hated even to visit cities, he said, because they "rumble at night"—and his idea of a good time was to wander his forest on foot, following the elephants that were his special passion: "I love them," he said. "Their size. Their gentleness. Their innocence.

"We are here for the animals," he added. "That is our duty." In performing that duty he had fought poachers hand-to-hand, survived a plot to frame him for murder, spurned offers of bribes to open up his forest for profit, and earned for himself a conservation award from the New York Zoographical Society.

"There is *no* grazing in my forest," he said. "*No* tree-cutting. And *no* poaching."

Ullas Karanth believes Nagarahole may well enjoy the highest density of hooved prey species in Asia. Night sounds provided perhaps the most eloquent evidence of Chinnappa's success. Diane and I bedded down in one of a cluster of thatched huts, built beneath a stand of magnificent teak trees whose big dry leaves blanketed the ground, and were lulled to sleep by the gentle thrashing sounds made by the hooves of scores of chital, huddling there after dark for protection from predators.

A couple of hours later, I sat bolt upright as the chital began racing in terrified circles and the forest exploded with alarm calls. A tiger was circling the clearing, roaring every hundred yards or so. Behind him padded a pack of jackals, howling their impatience that he had not yet provided them with a meal—and bringing back for me a thousand boyhood nights in Delhi.

## CHAPTER SIX

# THE RAJPUT

*S oda Lao!"* When Fateh Singh Rathore wants his servant to bring him soda water with which to dilute the Peter Scott whiskey he pours freely for the guests who flock to his terrace most evenings, the huge voice with which he demands it rattles off the hills of Ranthambhore that rise behind his handsome sandstone farmhouse and, it sometimes seems, must be audible in the bazaars of Sawai Madhopur, several miles away.

For more than a quarter of a century now, Fateh has been a resident of Ranthambhore. He has lived within its forested heart as a ranger, mapped and built its roads as wildlife warden, successfully shifted twelve villages from it as field director, nearly lost his life defending it against outsiders intent upon its destruction, and helped to document for the first time the secret lives of the tigers whose astonishing openness his efforts made possible.

If Ranthambhore was Project Tiger's most conspicuous success, Fateh Singh Rathore was its most successful—and most conspicuous—field director.

His thunderous voice is a legacy of his Rajput grandfather, Rai-Bahadur Laxman Singh Rathore, the *thakur,* or feudal ruler, of Chordiyan Village in the Rajasthan Desert near Jodhpur. A distinguished soldier in World War I, who rose from ordinary sepoy to *Rissaldar* and won a chestful of medals, the old man is said to have possessed a voice so loud that the inkpots and penholders and waterglasses in nearby offices rattled when he bellowed orders on the parade ground, so commanding that when he shouted for silence from the roof of his village house in the evening even infants thought better of crying, so sonorous that when he intoned the sacred syllable, *"Om,"* during his private devotions it echoed within every home. Laxman Singh is said to have been powerful enough to lift a camel calf above his head, and at the annual *Dussehra* observances, held by the Maharaja of Jodhpur atop the fortified hill in the center of his city, he could be counted upon to decapitate the sacrificial buffalo with a single blow of his sword, thus ensuring an auspicious new year for the princely Rathore clan to which he was honored to belong.

If Billy Arjan Singh can be said to represent something of the vanished British Raj, Fateh Singh Rathore is the product of feudal Rajasthan. He is *of* India, not merely living in it; a Rajput, the inheritor of a Hindu warrior tradition that emphasized dash and valor and devotion to duty as well as unalloyed pleasure in merriment of every kind.

Though he is in his late fifties now and a series of disappointments has begun to slow him down, Fateh still struts rather than walks, still gives his now-white mustache a wicked upturn, breaks often into song and dance. He remains the most vitally alive person I know—impulsive, bursting with energy, amused by almost everything (himself most of all), yet ready to weep the moment one of the lugubrious Urdu *ghazls* that are his favorite form of music begins keening from his stereo.

Rajasthan's history has traditionally been left to court bards, gifted storytellers whose reputation rested on their ability not only to recall what had happened but also to fashion it into a story filled with heroes and heroines and compelling enough

*Opposite:* A tigress that Fateh Singh Rathore and Valmik Thapar named Nick Ear dozes atop a *chatri*, part of the long-deserted Rajbagh Palace at Ranthambhore.

to hold new generations of listeners spellbound. To the bards of Rajasthan, objective facts have never been especially useful unless they happened to propel the story forward and, since Fateh is his own cheerful chronicler, I cannot attest to the absolute truth of everything I've been told about his early life (though the fact that he is so often the butt of his own tales provides at least some reassurance).

He is not sure precisely how old he is. His official birth date—August 10, 1938—is a "fake," he says, invented by his grandfather to satisfy some overinquisitve *babu* when he was first enrolled in school. But he does know that at the moment word came of his birth, his grandfather was being shaved by the village barber, who had the temerity to ask for *bakshish* to mark the propitious occasion. The indignant old man chased him through the village waving a stick, his chin still covered with lather, shouting, "Is my son a *eunuch* that I should celebrate his son's birth? I expect no less!"

Fateh's father was certainly not a eunuch—four more sons and four daughters followed—but he played a relatively small role in his son's life, in part because a Rajput father is by tradition supposed to be stern and uncomplimentary with the boy he values most, but also, perhaps, because he had himself been pulled out of school by his father after just four years, Laxman Singh having decreed that he would require no more education than that to manage the family lands. As a result, Fateh told me, "my father was *too* simple," a village *thakur* content with the fealty of those who lived in the village he would inherit from his father but uninterested in seeking success on his own beyond its confines.

From the first, his eldest son would feel differently. Fateh is steeped in the culture of his ancestors, a compendium of Rajput verse and song, aphorisms and folklore, but he seems always to have been eager to experience other worlds, certain that he was destined for greater things—though just what they would be remained murky for what seemed to his family an alarmingly long time.

Fateh was cherished by his mother as only an Indian mother can cherish a first-born son, but she also taught him the stoicism suitable to the descendant of warriors: When, as a very small boy, he expressed his terror of the ghosts said to dwell within a *khedaji* tree near their house, she marched him out one night and made him embrace its trunk so that he could see for himself that no harm would come to him. "You need fear nothing and no one," she told him, again and again.

No one, that was, except his grandfather, whose rule was as absolute as his habits were regular. Laxman Singh rose before dawn each day, downed a warm tumbler of *ghee* (clarified butter) spiced with a fistful of peppercorns, bathed at the well, then dispensed justice beneath a tree till lunchtime. "It didn't matter if he was right or wrong," Fateh recalls. "He was the *Thakur-sahib*." In the evening, another big meal was followed by prayers and bed. (When, late in life, the Jodhpur Maharaja's own physician warned the old man that his arteries were clogged, that if he wished to go on living he would have to eat only vegetables, he said he would rather die—and did.)

Laxman Singh was both traditional and tyrannical, and at least once his grandson felt his wrath. When the village pandit complained that the boy was doodling on his slate rather than learning the Hindi letters the priest was being paid to teach him, the old man seized his grandson by the arm and hurled him across the courtyard. But the old soldier had also seen something of the outside world and was ambitious for all his male descendants except his eldest son. Fateh's two uncles were sent away to

Fateh Singh Rathore comes face to face with two of the tigers whose survival was due largely to his vigilance.

school and college, then such a rare occurrence in Rajasthan that when the first boy returned with his degree, the Maharaja sent a brass band to the Jodhpur railroad station to welcome him home. Sultan Singh distinguished himself as a soldier in World War II, then went on to become Inspector General of Police in Rajasthan; Khet Singh practiced law and became a prominent Congress Party politician. Each would play an important part in furthering Fateh's career.

The old man's dreams for his first grandson were lofty, too. Before the boy was four, the old man determined to send him to boarding school at Baleshwar, one and a half days away across the desert. Fateh's mother held back her tears as the little boy left home: "If you want to be a human being," she told him, "you must learn about the world." Laxman Singh himself took his grandson to school by camel. Fateh slept part of the way, strapped tightly to his grandfather's chest by the old man's pistol belt; a jagged scar still visible across his nose was caused by the swaying of the camel and the chafing of that belt.

Fateh attended several schools, living with his uncles between terms, growing accustomed to a far richer life than he had ever known in his village. He was brash but charming, thoroughly spoiled—and without a clue as to what he might do with his life. While attending college in Udaipur, he ignored his studies in favor of amateur theatricals, fell in love first with a college actress, then with a politician's daughter, talked airily of going to Bombay and trying his luck as a comic actor in the movies.

Appalled, Sultan Singh told him he must abandon any such notion: he was a Rajput, and had to find something more in keeping with his martial ancestry. He was pushed into the Navy. Fateh liked the showy side of the service—"all those pips around your shoulders"—but he was a son of the desert, unable to swim and desperately seasick. Six months of sea duty aboard a cruiser proved to be "torture"; he quarreled with an officer, and it was only with difficulty that his uncle winkled him out of the service without a court-martial.

He then moved in with his other uncle, Khet Singh, already a prominent Jodhpur lawyer, who urged a career in law and politics. Fateh dutifully enrolled in law school at night, then took a day job tending store to earn pocket money. Nothing worked. He liked chatting up the customers, but quickly grew bored keeping stock of crockery and bangles and brassieres; eventually his uncle had to pay the shop owner some 25,000 rupees in lost profits. Worse, it had taken Fateh just two classes to see that the confines of the courtroom were not for him, a conviction he managed to keep to himself for a full year, pretending to attend class while using the fees his uncle gave him to buy movie tickets.

When Khet Singh got over his disappointment that his amiable but ne'er-do-well nephew would not be following in his footsteps, he sighed and obtained for him instead a licence to sell soft coal brought in from Bihar by rail. At first, things went well. Fateh arranged for the delivery of three boxcars of coal a week, all the local market would bear. Then for several weeks no coal arrived. Customers complained. Fateh sent telegram after telegram to Bihar, demanding to know what had happened. Finally, to his horror, an entire coal train pulled into the station—some fifty boxcars of coal, sixteen times more than he could hope to sell. By the time he had paid to have it all unloaded and stored, he had cost the family another 50,000 rupees. "It was a disaster," Fateh remembers. "I was a disaster."

His father and uncles held a family council. The boy was clearly out of control. Maybe marriage would straighten him out. Fateh was against it: he was not ready to get married. His mother agreed: "My jewel," he remembers her saying, "will be broken with a stone." But the elders won out, and without even the opportunity to see a photograph, Fateh was married off to a lovely stranger named Khem Kanwar. Meanwhile, Khet Singh had become the Deputy Minister of Forests in the Rajasthan government and could offer his newly married nephew still another job—this time as a ranger in the Forest Department. Fateh's first thought at the time, he remembers, was "Fantastic! Now I'll be an outdoor man!"

Fateh's interest in the natural world grew painfully slowly. "I was more interested in riding my English Royal Enfield motorcycle than caring for animals in those days," he recalls, and he is full of stories of his own initial ignorance of how the jungle worked. A tiger whose curiosity about the sound of his motorcycle drew him out onto the roadside to investigate sent Fateh scrambling up a tree where he perched, trembling, for better than an hour. A winter's evening spent with a fellow ranger, shivering in blankets while sawing on a string tied to a goat's ear in the hope that the animal's irritated bleating might lure a man-eating tiger within rifle range, ended badly: When a hungry leopard slipped up behind them instead of the tiger, and Fateh lit a cigarette, the leopard roared in fright and took off in one direction, the frantic goat raced away in another, Fateh and his companion in a third.

The most memorable event of his early years in the forest service came in 1960, when he was called to Ranthambhore from his first post at Sariska, to help organize a beat for the Maharaja of Jaipur that brought a big male tiger past the sights of the Duke of Edinburgh's rifle. (A persistent rumor around Sawai Madhopur holds that a second tiger, a female, was shot that same day by the queen herself, but that everyone subsequently thought it best that it not be reported to the press for fear of riling animal lovers back home.)

But slowly, almost imperceptibly, Fateh's views began to change. He spent brief periods elsewhere: at Sariska for a time, and at Mount Abu, where his son Goverdhan was born in 1964. (Two daughters, Padmini and Jaya, would follow before his marriage foundered.) The forests of Ranthambhore provided him with a peace he had never encountered before; he grew more and more intrigued by the intricacies of its bird and animal life, and, like Billy Arjan Singh, began to resent the seasonal presence of hunters who paid handsomely for the privilege of shooting at his charges. Once, when he spotted *shikaris* building a *machan* so that yet another pair of American clients could sit up for a tiger, he decided to intervene. During the day he managed quietly to plant a rounded stone at the bottom of the tree, painted orange as if it were an object of religious worship. Then, after dark, with the buffalo firmly tied and the two foreigners seated on their platform, rifles at the ready, he and a group of forest guards willing to go along with the gag emerged from the forest, ringing bells, beating drums and loudly chanting *bhajans* (prayers set to music) to the forest deity Fateh had fabricated. No tiger came anywhere near the bait. The Americans left the next morning, stiff and sleepless, muttering about the credulity of Indians.

Ranthambhore was a very different place in those days. The massive old fort still dominated the landscape, of course, and handsome ruins were scattered everywhere, but there were also sixteen villages within the forest, home to some fifteen hundred people who tilled fields and tended perhaps ten thousand head of voracious cattle. The few surviving tigers ventured out to hunt only at night; Fateh rarely saw them more than two or three times a year, and did not then expect that anyone would ever see them more often.

He was still a fairly conventional junior officer, happier than most of his colleagues to be in the forest, and unable to resist the sort of prank that had spoiled the Americans' *shikar*, but still without much real ambition for himself or for his park.

Then, in 1969, he was picked to take a diploma course in wildlife at the newly established Wildlife Institute at Dehra Dhun. It took him some time to buckle down—it all seemed alarmingly reminiscent of college, he remembers—but he did well in the

A tigress and her cub
end an afternoon's sleep
at Ranthambhore.

end, largely thanks to two people who insisted that he raise his sights. One was the course director, S. R. Choudhury, a much-admired authority on tigers, who was impressed by Fateh's energy and intelligence, and exhorted him to focus both on the forest he loved best, to "work and live for Ranthambhore."

The other was an elderly Englishwoman named Diana Wordsworth, to whom he was introduced by a mutual friend. A widowed relative of the poet William Wordsworth, she had lost all the members of her immediate family before she arrived in India, fell in love with a retired cavalry officer, and resolved to stay on and make a new life with him. Big and raw-boned—she once described herself as "the dried-up Englishwoman with the dominating voice"—and fond of heavy village silver and brightly colored Rajasthani skirts and blouses, she began calling herself Fateh's "Godmother," and took it upon herself to make something of the exuberant young Rajput who barely reached her shoulder but evidently came to represent for her the son she had never had.

Without the woman he still remembers as "Diana-Madame," Fateh says, he could never have accomplished what he accomplished at Ranthambhore. "She inspired me for all these things," he remembers. "She lifted me up and took me to England." (Actually, Fateh can be said to have taken her, since they drove overland and he did most of the driving behind the wheel of her white Land Rover.) It was she who first introduced him to the West, who insisted he see for himself how parks and sanctuaries were run in Britain, who gave him his first camera because, she said, she had the feeling Ranthambhore would one day present him with opportunities to photograph things no one had ever documented before.

And she preached ceaselessly the importance of doing the best possible job, of staying true to oneself, of rising above the corruption and influence-peddling and bureaucratic inertia that too often corrodes government service. Ranthambhore was a magical place, she told him; it was his duty to see to its protection. He must be all that he could be.

Fateh listened and learned, finding confirmation for convictions he had already begun to develop for himself, even as he taught Diana the facts of life in India. He found her a cook-bearer, saw that the contractor who built her house at Mount Abu did not make much more money off her than he should have, handled negotiations with local officials on the prowl for bribes.

And he taught her harder lessons, too. Driving on the outskirts of Alwar with Fateh late one evening, she accidentally hit and killed a donkey that lunged suddenly onto the road. A crowd began to gather.

Fateh urged her to drive on: "Come on, let's go."

She wouldn't hear of it. She had to find the owner, she said; must apologize and pay compensation for the loss.

"Okay, Madame," Fateh said. "But you'll have big problem. I know my country."

She insisted. Fateh rolled down the window and asked if anyone knew who had owned the dead donkey.

An elderly woman stepped forward and began to weep; it had been hers, she said, all that she owned.

Diana paid her several hundred rupees, patted her shoulder in sympathy.

Less than a hundred yards further on, an elderly man stepped in front of the Land Rover. Diana stopped. It was *his* donkey that had been killed, the old man said. He wanted money.

Diana reluctantly opened her purse. He took the rupee notes without a word.

She started the engine.

Five men now lay across the road. "My donkey!" one began to wail. "You killed my donkey!"

"Bloody country!" Diana said, banging her fist on the steering wheel.

Fateh, roaring now with glee, led her to the police station where a close friend was in charge. He saw that all the money was returned to her. The donkey had belonged to no one.

In 1970—the year tiger shooting was finally banned in India, the year before the leopard Prince arrived at Tiger Haven and transformed Billy's life—Fateh was promoted to wildlife warden at Ranthambhore and began to work in earnest for its future. He labored to win the trust of the villagers; released crocodile fingerlings into the lakes; supervised the transformation of a crumbling lakeside ruin into the splendid Jogi Mahal; and began walking the forest with a small band of forest guards, laying out the beginnings of a serpentine network of dirt roads—"the veins of my park," he calls them—which would one day total more than two hundred kilometers and allow him to keep track of what was happening in its most remote sections.

Valmik Thapar, fresh from a day's drive in the jungle.

In January 1976, a tall, bearded, hollow-eyed young man from New Delhi turned up at Fateh's office in Sawai Madhopur, asking whether he might be allowed to spend a few days at the Jogi Mahal. He was in flight from a marriage that had suddenly gone sour and some time in the forest, he thought, might help him feel better. His name was Valmik Thapar.

Fateh let him stay. Neither man's life would ever be the same again. On the surface, Valmik seems an implausible Tiger-Wallah. Neither a former hunter nor a forest officer, he grew up—and still lives part of the time—in a comfortable house less than five hundred yards from the one in which I and my family had lived in Delhi during the fifties, and his remarkable parents, Romesh and Raj Thapar, were radical intellectuals whose walls were hung with Indian art and whose dinner-table talk revolved around politics and art and the academy, not tigers. Valmik himself was a recent graduate of St. Stephen's College with a degree in social anthropology and plans for becoming a maker of documentary films.

On his first visit to Ranthambhore, it took him nearly three weeks of driving up and down the roads at night before he got even a fleeting look at a tiger, but that one glimpse—"the unmistakable glow of the striped coat," he has written, "the powerful, unhurried, silent walk …"—was enough to hook and hold him.

He returned again and again over the next few months, finding both solace and excitement in an environment utterly unlike the one in which he had been raised, and discovering in Fateh's gregarious high spirits and boundless enthusiasm a badly needed antidote for his own grief and inbred reticence.

Even though Ranthambhore was now a Project Tiger Reserve, weeks still went by without a visitor, and Fateh welcomed Valmik as an eager disciple whose fascination with the forest soon rivaled his. Together, the two men began to study Ranthambhore's still rarely seen tigers—following pug marks along the dusty roads by day, driving through the forest with spotlights after dark, then sipping whiskey at the Jogi Mahal, discussing what they had or hadn't seen and how they might improve the park while the sparks flew upward and bats flitted in and out of the firelight.

If Ranthambhore was ever to be restored to anything like the wilderness it once had been, both men knew, the dozen villages that were scattered through the heart of the park would somehow have to be shifted out. The villagers did not want to move. The life they led within Ranthambhore was meager and marginal—their herds were scrawny, the land they farmed stony and exhausted—but for more than two centuries it was all they and their ancestors had known.

Fateh could have resorted to force: it was the time of Indira Gandhi's Emergency, civil liberties had largely been suspended, and the close alliance he had carefully forged with the local collector and the superintendent of police would have provided all the armed backing he needed. (Some years later, when herdsmen were barred from the Kaladeo bird sanctuary that now occupies the broad artificial lake where the Maharajas of Bharatpur once organized their annual slaughter of wildfowl, there was an angry confrontation with the local police that left five villagers dead and thirty-five more wounded.)

Instead, he relied on patience and persuasion. He was authorized to offer each householder financial compensation as well as more land than he now owned, provided he agreed to move to a new site outside the sanctuary. There would be new schools, temples, access to a post office, a modern well and electricity with which to pump its precious water. If the villagers were wary of government promises, he told them, they should hold him personally responsible for making good on them; like his feudal ancestors, he would do all he could for them so long as he was in charge.

But mixed in with these material incentives was a spiritual message as well: The forest and all its creatures were the creation of the gods, he argued over the village fires. Did not the goddess Durga, the slayer of demons, herself ride a tiger? No man had a right to disturb that divine creation. The forests must be left to grow back, to become again what their creator had intended. To continue to live in the forest, cutting its trees, devouring its foliage, was to commit a kind of blasphemy.

One by one, the villagers agreed to go, though sometimes it was a close thing. Valmik was present one evening when, with district officials present armed with cash with which to begin paying compensation, the people of Lahpur, the largest of all the villages in the park, suddenly balked: they did not want money or additional land, they said, they just wanted to go on living where they had always lived.

Again, Fateh applied tact and patience. For three hours, seated at their fire, he did his best to calm the villagers' fears about the new kind of life they would have to learn to live outside the park, and he agreed that they could remain in their homes until their last crop had been harvested.

When the day for them to move finally came, and trucks drew up to carry their belongings to their new homes, many wept. One old man hugged a gnarled tree, crying that his father and grandfather had rested at its roots, and a tearful old woman pleaded to be allowed to stay behind so that after she died she might be reborn as a peacock beneath the trees that shaded the only world she had ever known.

The villagers' misery and fear was so palpable that Valmik, watching from the sidelines and knowing that the future of the forest depended on their removal, still could not keep himself from crying. Neither could Fateh, but he made sure they went.

By 1979, all twelve villages were gone from the heart of the park (four still remain just inside the park's fringes), and soon, except for the intermittent, spooky blare of conch shells blown by the sadhus who continued to live on, hidden in their ravine, Ranthambhore was left to the birds and animals—more than 270 species of the former, 22 of the latter.

For Fateh, everything in the park still seems "fantastic"—the animals, the feathery *dhok* trees, even the ubiquitous vultures. Only the big crocodiles strain his affection. They take hours to kill the sambar they sometimes seize, he says, breaking first one leg, then another, biting off the tail, the ears, while the pinioned animals shriek with fear and pain. "Sometimes you want to shoot to end their misery," he says. "But you must not. Nature takes care of everything. Nothing must interfere with it."

That simple policy was the secret of Fateh's success at Ranthambhore. He ended baiting and night driving within the park—though it won him few friends among visiting politicians and other VIPs who were no longer guaranteed to see a tiger. Under his benign neglect, farmers' fields quickly turned back into tangled forest and deer nuzzled through the deserted villages; but the outer walls of some old huts still stood, and one day not long before Diane and I paid our first visit to Ranthambhore in

*Pages 116–117:*
The tigress Laxmi (foreground)—daughter of the tigress with which Fateh Singh Rathore and Valmik Thapar began their study—and three of her cubs sleep off the meal they have just made of a sambar hind.

1983, Fateh took the headman of one of the old villages back to see its transformed site. A tiger lay sleeping in one of the ruined houses. The headman was delighted. "Now we are happy," he said. "The goddess has come."

The forest flourished in the absence of human beings, yet the villagers' departure presented Fateh with a new and largely unforeseen challenge as well. Ranthambhore's villagers had always jealously guarded their forest against encroachment by those living outside the park. Now, with its traditional guardians gone, herdsmen from the surrounding countryside began driving their animals inside. If the forest no longer belonged to specific villages, they reasoned, it must belong to everyone.

Protection was left to Fateh and his forest guards. There were violent confrontations, pitched battles, and in October 1981, some fifty villagers armed with clubs cornered Fateh on the border of the park. "They decided to give me a good beating," he remembers. In fact, they left him for dead: kneecap shattered, nose broken, skull fractured. Only the bravery of his driver, who threw his own body across that of his chief, saved his life.

Fateh spent three months in the hospital and eventually received the World Wildlife Fund's International Valor Award for bravery in the field. Friends advised him to leave Ranthambhore; his own mother, who had taught him to fear nothing, told him she feared for his life if he went back there. But he did go back—to Ranthambhore, and to the very village from which his attackers came, driving into its center while still in plaster casts and challenging its residents to try again. "I wanted them to see I was still alive," he remembers, "that they had done the wrong thing, but I was still willing to work together with them." (That is Fateh's retrospective view of what he had in mind. A close friend of his recalls being given a somewhat more aggressive version of his return to action. "All you men who have drunk your mother's milk," he was reported to have shouted, "come out. I am here!" Then he tied several of their bullock carts to his jeep and clattered off with them down the road. Tact has never been Fateh's strong suit.)

B y the late 1980s there were said to be upward of forty tigers within the park—and the leopards that were once seen with some frequency in its heart had been pushed outward to its rocky fringes by their bigger, more powerful rivals.

But it was the unusual boldness of the Ranthambore tigers, not merely their numbers, that made their park the showpiece of Project Tiger. Like tigers elsewhere, they had always remained creatures of the night, secretive and shy, taught from infancy that they must avoid all contact with human beings. "Tigers are naturally diurnal," Valmik believes. "They became nocturnal only out of fear of man. Remove that fear, and they revert to their natural behavior."

Thanks to Fateh's vigilance and to the gradual removal of human encroachment, he argues, new generations of tigers were soon being born at Ranthambhore to mothers that had never heard a shot fired, had never experienced aggression by men, and therefore saw little need to teach their offspring to be fearful of them.

It began in 1977 with a tigress that Fateh had named for his eldest daughter, Padmini. A peppering of tiny pug marks around her big ones had told him that she had given birth to five cubs sometime the previous year. But for months, try as he might, he was unable to get even a glimpse of them.

Then, just after dusk one evening, not far from the site of one of the first villages to be abandoned, he caught Padmini snarling in his headlights and behind her saw five ten-month-old cubs race across the road and into the undergrowth.

He was transfixed. The sight of the first tiger family he had ever seen after almost twenty years spent living in their midst, he remembered, "put me *in love* with tigers."

Billy Arjan Singh most admires the tiger's power and its ability to live and prosper utterly on its own. Fateh is drawn by something else. "Power is boring to me," he says. "I know too much about it. A *thakur* is supposed to look powerful. He's supposed to frown a lot. Even his mustache is meant to frighten people. I never wanted that. If power was all that tigers had, I would not care for them. Tigers are so *beautiful. That's* the whole point."

He rushed to town, sent a telegram to Delhi urging Valmik to come as soon as he could, then hurried back to the forest where he spent the better part of five days in a tree watching Padmini sit beside a kill to which her cubs came only at night. She objected strenuously to his presence at first, charging the tree twice in hopes of driving Fateh off. But he stayed put, clicking his camera while trying to reassure himself as she roared beneath him that grown tigers only "rarely" climb trees. After a time, she seemed to resign herself to his presence and eventually largely ignored it even when her cubs were present, provided he kept his distance.

The frailest of her cubs, a female, soon died, but Fateh and Valmik spent more than a year, off and on, observing and recording in photographs Padmini and her four surviving offspring. They learned to tell them apart by their distinctive facial markings, gave them names—Akbar and Babar and Hamir and Laxmi—watched in fascination as their mother taught them to hunt, and fretted terribly when the time came for the cubs to leave her for fear they would not be able to survive on their own.

They all did survive, however, and in 1981, Laxmi gave birth to three cubs of her

A sated tiger sleeps; anyone who regularly observes tigers in the wild spends an astonishing amount of time just waiting for the objects of their surveillance to wake up.

own. The cubs were less than three months old when Valmik came upon them half-hidden in a bush—the size of large housecats but endearingly clumsy, with oversized heads and paws. At Fateh's first glimpse of them, he burst into tears.

Valmik asked him why he was crying.

"The *happiness* is there," he said. "It has to come out."

It had all been worthwhile—the hard, lonely labor, the delicate negotiations that had persuaded the inhabitants of a dozen villages to abandon their ancestral homes, his encounters with the graziers, his struggles with bureaucrats and poachers and intrusive VIPs.

Fateh is not conventionally religious. "I don't believe in all that *tamasha* [spectacle]," he says, "gods, goddesses, statues, this, that. But I do believe in a Creator and I'm possibly put here to do one job—save the animals. Ultimately, that's what I'm meant to do."

Thanks to his dedication to doing that job, observers were able to watch closely for the first time in history as one generation of a tiger family in the wild gave way to the next. And there were more revelations to come. Over the next few years, Fateh and Valmik would follow the lives led by three different tiger families, documenting for the first time that at Ranthambhore, at least, male tigers—traditionally thought inveterate loners that kill even their own offspring if they happen upon them—actually nuzzled and played with their cubs and sometimes shared with them their kills.

Such intimate and prolonged observations of tigers in the wild had never been possible before, and in 1983, Valmik and Fateh produced *With Tigers in the Wild*, the first of four richly illustrated, groundbreaking books on tiger behavior.

It was not long before visitors from all over the world began turning up at the park gates, eager to see for themselves what Fateh and Valmik had shown them on paper—and to meet the Tiger-Wallahs, too.

Both men found themselves celebrities, something which Valmik found excruciating and Fateh thoroughly enjoyed. "My tigers have made me an international man," Fateh once told me with a broad grin, and his sudden prominence—along with his distinctive Stetson and safari clothes—began to grate on other members of the Forest Department less charismatic (and less dedicated) than he. Other people were

Cubs try out their killing techniques on an uncooperative Ranthambhore peahen.

Cubs display all the
signs of having finished
a good meal.

annoyed, too—some of them rich men and politicians to whom he had been insuffi-ciently obsequious and a handful of whom he had actually arrested for poaching. As Fateh's fame and the fame of his park began to grow together, so did the list of his envious critics.

Traditionally, tourists hoping to see tigers had had to content themselves with bril-liant flashes of black and orange disappearing into dense undergrowth. Here, in this unrivaled setting, almost every aspect of their lives now lay open to the patient visi-tor's gaze.

In fact, Ranthambhore made it easy to lose sight of the fact that while tigers are beautiful, they are never cuddly. I once spent a whole afternoon watching four tigers sleep off a meal. They were dozing in the shade; I was sitting in the sun. No human sound seemed to disturb them: our restless shifting in the jeep had no effect on the loud, steady, bellowslike sound of their breathing, neither did the voices of a road crew passing in the distance, nor a series of blasts from a rock quarry outside the park. After the third hot, drowsy hour, it was all I could do to stop myself from getting down to sleep alongside them. Then, the gentle flutter of a tree-pie's wings hopping too close to the kill brought the tigress roaring to her feet—and me to my senses. Even the minute threat to her kill offered by a small bird had demanded action; so might I have, had I actually got down. But sitting in the jeep, neither menace nor potential meal, I was just part of the landscape.

The tigers of Ranthambore proved not only audacious but adaptable. Some learned to exploit the jeep's noisy presence, shrewdly waiting to inch a little closer,

121

until the sudden stutter of an engine diverted their nervous quarry's attention. Along with the occupants of half a dozen other vehicles one evening, I watched a tigress take fifteen minutes to creep one hundred yards across open ground toward a dozen chital high on a hillside. She managed to move so stealthily, despite the lack of cover and the ceaseless clicking of cameras, that she alarmed neither the deer nor the normally clamorous peacocks congregated at the edge of the clearing. Then, she charged up the slope—only to miss her kill because, once actually among her clattering, terrified prey, she could not decide upon which animal to concentrate her attack until all had sprung out of reach. Mouth open, panting with exertion, she stalked slowly up and over the ridge, taunted by the calls of the belatedly indignant deer.

One massive male tiger that Fateh and Valmik named Genghis introduced in 1983 a method of killing never before observed anywhere else on earth. He routinely hid in the tall grass that lines the largest of the lakes, then stormed out into the water to snatch an unwary young sambar before it could make it back to solid ground—and he sometimes performed this spectacular feat in full view of guests sipping tea on the verandah of the Jogi Mahal.

Even more remarkable, perhaps, was the fact that after this innovator vanished the next year, his former companion, a tigress called Noon that had often watched Genghis charge into the water, began to employ the same theatrical technique.

Because of her fearlessness in the presence of visitors' vehicles and the fact that her range included the parts of the park nearest to Jogi Mahal and the main gate, Noon became perhaps the most frequently seen and most widely photographed wild

The tigress Noon lands a left paw to the head of an intrusive male, less than fifty feet from the vehicle from which they were photographed.

tiger in the world. She also played a central role in the most memorable encounter I was ever privilged to share with Fateh and Valmik and the tigers of Ranthambhore.

There were already three tigers half hidden in the tall yellow grass that surrounded us: Noon and her two nearly full-grown cubs. Fateh had guided us to them, his eyes searching both sides of the road for minute signs of their presence the unitiated would never otherwise have seen: A few displaced pebbles told him that a tiger had dragged its kill across the track; a single, agitated tree-pie, flying in and out of the grass, signaled where it was concealed.

Then, the deep, frenzied alarm call of a sambar hind warned of the arrival of still another tiger. Behind us and off to the left, a huge male appeared, weighing perhaps five hundred pounds, head down and padding steadily toward the open jeep in which we were all sitting very still.

Noon saw him coming, too, and sent her male cub bounding away to safety, his tail high in the air in understandable panic. Then she melted into the grass with her female offspring, away from the carcass of the sambar stag which she had killed and which we had been watching her and her cubs eat all morning.

The big male entered the grass, passing within twenty feet of the jeep and according us only a casually malevolent look, then settled heavily down to sleep next to the misappropriated kill.

Everything was quiet for a time, the only sound the buzzing of the flies. Then the tigress reappeared, creeping almost imperceptibly through the grass toward the sleeping intruder, precisely the way a kitten might stalk across your living-room rug, but on an infinitely more menacing scale. As she silently placed one foot after the other, her eyes never left the male's back. She came within ten yards of him, then five feet, then three ... and touched him with her paw.

The male awakened, roaring. Noon roared back. Both animals reared up on their hind legs, massive snarling heads and bared claws high above the grass. They sparred for a moment, then, with one blow, the male slapped the much smaller tigress down.

Her shoulder bleeding, she backed off meekly to the shade of the nearest tree to await another chance to feed. Peace returned, broken only by the male's gnawing of the sambar bones, the busy flies and the cawing of a far-off jungle crow.

When the male had finally had his fill, one of the big cubs approached the kill, appropriated the remnant of a leg and, apparently annoyed by the hot sun, brought it in his mouth under the fender of our Land Rover and began to feed, his face a mask of blood.

"This is a bit much," Thapar whispered, grinning. I could have leaned down and scratched the tiger behind the ears. Fateh, in the back, continued to click his camera's shutter. When no morsel remained, the cub returned to its mother's side and sprawled in the grass to sleep.

Later, attracted by the sweet, breeze-blown scent of the kill, three wild boar trotted busily toward the grass, then skittered to a stop at its edge as the fainter smell of the tiger reached them. The anxious pigs skipped forward, skittered back, advanced again, back hair bristling, wet uplifted snouts aquiver. Hunger and fear now competed—tiger kills are free meals for wild boar; wild boar are a favorite tiger food—and fear finally won out. All three wheeled and rushed off.

"Red letter day," said Valmik, as he started the engine and we drove off, leaving the tigers to their kill. "Red letter day."

## CHAPTER SEVEN

# STRESS OF CIRCUMSTANCES

Project Tiger's first decade ended in 1983. It seemed a spectacular success. The number of tigers inside and outside its reserves was said to have more than doubled, to 4,000, and there then seemed to be no end to the wonders the new preservation policies might achieve. The number of Indian national parks and sanctuaries was growing, too. In 1975, there had been just five national parks and 126 state sanctuaries in the whole country; those numbers have grown steadily since and as I write encompass more than 450—at least on paper—with still more being planned. Few countries have made a more resolute effort to preserve their native species in the face of almost overwhelming odds.

But as Project Tiger moved into the mid-eighties, it became increasingly clear that the same problems which threatened the well-being of India in general—massive, endemic corruption; bureaucratic paralysis; the politics of cynicism; a population growing wildly out of control; a lack of genuine concern for improving the plight of India's villagers; and the chronic inability of the state and central governments to work together—were combining to cripple its efforts at conserving forests and wildlife, as well.

The first signs of real trouble were already evident at Dudhwa where, beginning in the late seventies, there had been a startling rise in man-eating. Since this coincided roughly with Tara's release into the forest, local people who had always lived in fear of Billy's charges blamed his tigress for the deaths. Forest officials who should have known better found it politically expedient to blame her, too: freed of her innate fear of humans, they argued without any evidence, she must be approaching strangers and, when they failed to produce the food she had come to expect, killing them out of a combination of hunger and frustration. In 1980, the park director shot a tigress that had in fact killed three men within the park, then told the press it was Tara, and paraded the garlanded corpse through all the large towns between Palia and Lucknow. Thousands turned out to see the dead man-eater.

The park director said he intended the procession to provide the most vivid possible evidence that the Forest Department had the welfare of local people uppermost in its mind. To Billy, on the other hand, the noisy cross-country cavalcade was an obscenity, proof only of the fearful price exacted from tigers when human beings were allowed to invade the strongholds supposedly set aside for them.

Billy's ongoing war with the Forest Department is partly rooted in his own personality. While he has never met a predator he didn't like, the same cannot be said of the human beings he has encountered, especially those who wield power over him. From boyhood, he has loathed authority: he could not bear Army life because of it, was unwilling to submit to the day-to-day humiliations a life in business or government service would inevitably have required of him. Nor has he ever quite believed that rules made by others applied to him or, provided his cause was just, that a man should ever have to compromise. Like the great cats that are his passion, he is a loner, answerable to no one, and during his early years in Kheri that worked well for

*Opposite:* A tiger protects his kill, a sambar fawn, at Ranthambhore.

him. But when Dudhwa became a sanctuary and Billy could no longer rule it as his exclusive fiefdom, conflict was probably inevitable.

Running one of India's parks is a daunting job, and the private complaints of park directors seem to be the same everywhere. Forest staffs are small, poorly paid, and often poorly motivated. There are rarely enough vehicles or firearms for adequate patrolling. And there is a bewildering array of outsiders to placate—politicians with no understanding of how the forests work, superiors within the Forest Department interested only in hearing good news that will reflect well on them, journalists equally interested in uncovering bad news about the latest poaching scandal, local people with complaints about animals devouring their crops or preying on their livestock or their families.

Then, too, family life in the remote districts in which most parks are located is difficult; housing is often primitive and there are rarely good schools nearby. And (though this is rarely discussed openly) the management of wildlife provides comparatively few opportunities for amassing the kinds of illicit extra income that makes life in the state Forest Department's more lucrative commercial and "Social Forestry" wings so much more rewarding to an ambitious man.

Billy has never had much sympathy with such complaints. "Excuses, excuses," he says. "They can always tell you why they *can't* do things. Meanwhile, the parks die." To him, preserving wildlife has been a great privilege that lent meaning to his life, and he cannot comprehend how anyone, given the same opportunities to do good that he has had, should not feel the same sense of mission. Those unwilling to endure a little hardship for wildlife's sake, he feels, are dilettantes at best, corrupt frauds at worst. It is not an attitude calculated to win him friends among the forest staff.

In any case, the dead animal was not Tara, as a comparison between its distinctive facial markings and hers made perfectly clear, and an official, independent inquiry later confirmed that Billy's tigress was not guilty of having killed anyone. But the same inquiry also called a halt to any more efforts to reintroduce predators into the wild: such projects were too dangerous, it said, and there was a risk of genetic damage to the Indian species. And it hadn't worked, anyway: At the same time the committee found Tara blameless, it also pronounced her dead and decreed Billy's experiment a failure.

Stung, he determined to prove them wrong. Billy is certain that Tara lived on to bear four litters of cubs before finally disappearing from her range sometime in 1988, and he followed the almost daily fortunes of the tigress he believes had been his for eight years. But even some of Billy's most ardent admirers admit that the facial markings of the tigress he photographed so often look sufficiently different from those of the authentic Tara to raise at least a reasonable doubt that she could have been the same animal.

Twice, Billy showed me the tigress he was sure was Tara and called out her name in his distinctive voice. Each time she stopped what she was doing, peered intently in the direction from which the voice came, then withdrew into the forest. She did not seem as startled as an ordinary tiger would have been to hear a human being suddenly call out to her; but there was no way for me to know whether she acted so placidly because she actually recognized the voice of the man who had raised her, or had simply become accustomed to Billy's voice because she had heard it so often during his ceaseless monitoring of her activities.

Yet it did occur to me that had Billy ever proved conclusively that this was indeed

A cub, less than two months old, at Kanha.

his tigress—had she ever returned at the sound of his voice to rub her sides against his leg again, as he so obviously hoped she would—he might have won one battle with his antagonists within the Forest Department, but he would also have lost his war, since a tigress that had come back to him could surely not be said to have ever become wild at all.

In any case, there was no longer any hope of further reintroductions, and even Billy believed for a time that the steadily increasing number of tigers, within his park and elsewhere in India, might make them unnecessary.

In the mid-eighties not even Billy denied that there were a good many more tigers in the Indian jungles than there had been a decade earlier. Just how many more, however, was already a matter of some controversy. Tigers, for the most part, remain secretive, mostly solitary creatures—their survival depends on stealth and mobility, after all—and precise facts about them are hard to come by. An All-India Tiger Census is made every five years; it includes all national parks and state sanctuaries, plus an estimate of all the animals said to live in the degraded forests outside their precincts.

It is a considerable undertaking: Hundreds of thousands of square miles of forest scattered in patches all across the country are divided into equal-sized blocks; then, in a given week, each square is systematically crisscrossed by Forest Department employees who search for tiger pug marks while noting all the wildlife they see along the way. Some ten thousand men take part, equipped with glass plates on which they trace any prints found and record their location, the date, and the sort of ground on which they were discovered. Forest officers then compile the results and are supposed to be able to identify the sex and distinguishing features of each individual animal.

The bureaucratic completeness of these tallies is sometimes breathtaking: One park director boasted to me that he not only knew exactly how many tigers prowled his forest but the precise number of male and female mongoose and python living there, too. A forest guard at another park reported having spotted twenty-eight porcupines during a single day in the field; his superior thought this figure startlingly high and asked him to count aloud. He did so: "One, two, three, four, five, six, seven, (long pause) ... twenty-eight."

R. L. Singh, the former director of Project Tiger, admits that roughly half the men who took part in the census during his tenure had little or no training, and, although one former field director went so far as to claim that each tiger's footprints are as unique as are human fingerprints, many researchers question the whole notion of identification by pug mark. "It's all nonsense," Billy says. "I've been tracking tigers almost every day now for forty years and even I am unable to differentiate from pug marks alone between tigers of the same size and sex, unless there's some abnormality—and even that doesn't always show up." During one count at Dudhwa, some field workers solemnly turned in pug-mark tracings that had five toes—one more than tigers actually possess. And Ullas Karanth has showed that there are simply not enough prey species in many of the parks to support anything like the numbers of tigers their directors have claimed.

The numbers were inflated because the bureaucracy demanded it. A park director who reported that the number of his tigers had fallen off could count on angering his

Pages 128–129:
A tigress leads her cub across the Neora River, just behind Tiger Haven.

superiors, whose stewardship was then sure to be questioned in the state legislature and perhaps even in Parliament; better to claim a steady rise.

Still, there undeniably was an authentic rise, at least at first, and around Dudhwa the ordinary people of North Kheri District were paying a fearful price for it—and for the fact that no plan had ever been formulated to deal with the ghastly consequences. By the time I first began visiting Billy in 1987, some one hundred and fifty people had been killed by tigers in the district, and almost as many more had been mauled.

No one knows precisely how many human deaths tigers cause each year in India. According to Project Tiger officials, between fifty and sixty people died annually during the 1980s: twenty-five to thirty in the Sundarbans, the vast mangrove forest on the border between India and Bangladesh where man-eating has been inexplicably endemic since the 17th century; twenty to twenty-five more in Kheri District; and the rest scattered across the subcontinent. Some supposed tiger killings are surely murders conveniently disguised, as Billy argues; on the other hand, it seems just as likely that word of some authentic kills in remote areas never reaches the authorities.

Most killings are still simply cases of mistaken identity—accidents. Since long before the advent of firearms, tigers have been innately wary of humans on foot. Charles McDougal, the American tiger expert who has for many years conducted research in the Royal Chitwan Reserve in Nepal, described watching a large tiger from elephant-back at Bandhavgarh. The animal was utterly unconcerned for half an hour, he said, dozing in the warm winter sun, but woke up and slipped instantly into the undergrowth when a man suddenly appeared walking along a forest track fully four hundred yards away.

And even when a tiger is surprised on a kill it does not wish to abandon, it follows a fairly standardized routine to scare off anyone who ventures too close: First it gives a warning roar (I have heard this sound several times now, and always found it awesomely persuasive). Then it roars still louder. Then, if the intruder somehow *still* fails to back off, it may make a mock charge. Finally, as likely as not, it will turn and run rather than launch an all-out attack.

Human beings walking upright and sticking to forest roads are relatively safe, then; it is when they wander off into the undergrowth and begin to bend over, cutting grass or collecting firewood, so that they lose their distinctively human look, that the likelihood of tragic error seems to intensify. One afternoon Billy invited me along on his afternoon walk through the thick forest behind his home. Perhaps I would see for myself what the problem was.

I struggled to keep up with him as he paced ahead on his sturdy legs, one of the short, carved "tiger sticks" that are the only weapons he carries cradled in his arm. We ducked beneath branches, picked our way through mud, stepped over fallen logs and twisted roots.

It occurs to me that I should perhaps explain why one is willing—no, eager—to follow Billy, unarmed and on foot, into a forest ruled by tigers. His blithe rationale for believing in his own safety is simple enough: he thinks tigers recognize their benefactors, and therefore will never harm him. (This axiom survived a fairly severe test a few years back when Billy inadvertently stumbled as he started down a hillside toward a tiger that had only recently killed a cartman and mauled the shoulder of his own tracker, Suresh. Billy tried to stand his ground but had trouble keeping his footing on the pebbled slope, and the tiger launched five mock charges before Suresh gently told his boss that they really had better leave.) In any case, it is unclear how the benefactor theory could apply to the benefactor's friends from overseas.

Yet Diane and I have each followed Billy into dense grass twice as tall as we were to visit a tiger's kill just because he was interested in seeing it, and we have gone along, too, as he plunged through the grass directly toward the spot at the base of a tree where, because a langur in its branches was coughing its rage and peering directly downward, he was certain a tiger lay. (He was right, but the tiger hurried off well before we got there.)

We stumble along behind Billy, I think, in part because it seems such an honor to be asked to accompany him into a world we could otherwise never get to know, because the possibility of seeing a tiger seems worth running almost any risk, and because we don't wish ever to let him down. He is fearless and, for the moment at least, he gives us the chance to be fearless, too.

"There you are," Billy said, stopping suddenly and pointing straight ahead. Only a few yards away, but three-quarters hidden by the leaves, I could just make out the bent backs of three men cutting grass to clear a path. Even to me, their silhouettes looked like those of browsing deer.

"That's just one reason why mixed use won't work," Billy said. "Tigers and man cannot share space. It really is as simple as that."

Encounters between human beings and tigers are usually but not always fatal. I have met two survivors: A young Nepalese woman, mauled while cutting grass at Chitwan, who was still somehow ambulatory despite the two neat round holes left behind her ears when her attacker's canines pierced first her skull and then her brain; and Shiv Shankar, a grizzled sixty-three-year-old farmer who lived near Dudhwa and managed to endure *two* attacks by two different tigers, thereby surely qualifying for the *Guinness Book of World Records*. Flames from an overturned kerosene lamp scared one attacker off; the shouts of his horrified companions drove away the other. I asked him to what he attributed his astonishing survival. He thought for a long moment. "I have always drunk a great deal of milk," he said.

Why did man-eating start here at Dudhwa, I asked Billy, hoping to slow his head-long pace through the jungle with a question or two.

"It had to start somewhere," he answered, continuing to push through the under-growth. "This was the most ecologically vulnerable area."

Dudhwa has a special problem, he explained. Project Tiger reserves—Dudhwa became one in 1988—are meant to have a buffer zone, an area in which human intrusion is strictly limited in order to keep the core area inviolate. Dudhwa has never had one. Instead, cultivators were allowed to plant sugar right up to the forest edge, and sugar cane, so tall and so thickly grown that two men cutting it ten feet apart cannot see one another, strikes tigresses as ideal cover in which to bear and hide their cubs. The sugar becomes their home then, and when, at harvest time, the cutters move into it, they defend it fiercely.

Later, accompanied by Billy and Kishan Chand, the youthful official who then headed the chronically undermanned local Tiger Watch, meant to monitor the activities of tigers throughout the district, I traveled to the scene of just such an encounter. It had been three weeks since a tigress had killed eighteen-year-old Rajesh Kumar on the outskirts of the village of Govindanagar, but the earth where he had lain after he was dragged into the sugar cane was still dark with blood, and we could hear in his grandfather's voice the horror he felt at having found his body.

A cautionary reminder of the recurring confrontations between animals and man, daubed on a village wall in Bihar.

It had been early morning, the old man said, and he had sent his grandson into the fields to shoo birds from the freshly planted wheat. When the boy failed to answer repeated calls to breakfast, he set out to look for him. At first he seemed simply to have vanished. Then the old man spotted his sandals, and saw scuff marks leading into the tall, thickly planted cane.

He parted the thicket, bent forward, and peered inside. His grandson lay sprawled on his back. Crouched just behind the corpse was the tigress, growling steadily. The grandfather fled, and by the time he returned with several of the more intrepid men from his village, the tigress had abandoned her kill and slipped away into the cane.

Had the tigress been seen since she had killed the boy, Billy asked as we walked back toward the village.

No, a tall Sikh said, but her big pug marks and those of her two cubs had been seen several times, scattered through the fields.

Everyone was frightened, a grizzled Muslim added. No one dared stir outside his hut after dark.

String beds were pulled into the center of the village path for the distinguished visitors to recline upon. Government officials rarely visit Govindanagar. Neither do foreigners, or famous men like Billy Arjan Singh.

The village headman was sent for. Brass tumblers of fresh buffalo milk were pushed into our hands. A small boy brought fruits and a plate of milk sweets. Everyone was very polite as Kishan Chand explained to the grieving old man how he should go about applying for compensation from the Forest Department for his loss. He was entitled to 10,000 rupees (then about $625). Had the boy been a minor, his loss would have brought only 5,000 rupees; a buffalo was worth 3,000, a cow just 800; in other Indian states the rates are often far lower, and in some, nonexistent. A man convicted of killing a tiger, on the other hand, must pay a fine of 5,000 rupees and serve six months in jail.

As the talk continued, a very old woman tottered along the path toward us. Too ancient to be thought immodest if she allowed herself to be looked upon by strangers, she stopped to listen. Then, suddenly, she began to shout in a strident, cracked voice from behind the corner of her sari: "Government cares *nothing* for us. It only cares about tigers. They should kill all the tigers before we are all killed."

The men looked sheepish. Some smiled. She had spoken out of turn, but she had also spoken for many of them.

Billy did his best to placate her. In the old days, he reminded his listeners, when the villages were few and there were still substantial stands of forest, tigers were seen as nightwatchmen for their fields, their steady threat a reliable deterrent to the deer and wild boar that now routinely devoured the crops. Some of the older men nodded agreement.

But now the forest had dwindled to virtually nothing—the ragged patch of trees from which the errant tigress and her cubs had evidently strayed was a kilometer or so away across the fields, and little larger than a neighborhood park in some American city. What were the animals to do?

The younger men smiled pleasantly but they did not nod. It would not have done for them to show disrespect toward an elder, but they had no such pleasant memories to comfort them.

Later, speeding back toward Billy's home in his battered Land Rover, I asked how long it would take for the old man to get his compensation.

"More than a year, once all the paperwork is done," Kishan Chand said. "That is a big part of the problem."

"Justice delayed is justice denied," Billy muttered, and that was not the worst of it. Bureaucratic corruption added to the tragedy. In order finally to get his small sum, the dead boy's grandfather would likely have to promise parts of it to a whole chain of greedy, better-educated men, ranging from the scribe who filled out his application forms and the bank clerk whose initials were required to cash his check to the Forest Department clerk whose cooperation was necessary before the old man's file reached the desk of the official authorized to issue it and, quite possibly, that official himself. Many victims forego the whole business rather than subject themselves to so many clamorous demands.

The tiger's champions like to point out that one hundred times more people die in India annually of snakebite than from tiger attacks; that the risk of a mauling is no greater to a villager living on the edge of a national park than is, say, a traffic accident to an American commuter. They are statistically correct; tiger attacks are still rare.

But to the family and friends of a tiger victim, statistics don't mean much, and grief is easily transformed into anger. In 1986 and 1987 alone, in and around Dudhwa, twenty-five tigers died in mysterious circumstances: one had its head blown off by a bomb planted in its kill; a forest guard was found burning the corpse of another tiger rather than have his superiors find out that one of his charges had been done in; and Billy himself came upon the skeleton of a third surrounded by the reeking corpses of some one hundred and fifty vultures—someone had poisoned the tiger's kill, the tiger had eaten from it and died, and the poison remaining in his body, in turn, had done in the overeager scavengers that fell upon it. After several dead tigers were found floating in canals and lying along railroad tracks, a local politician claimed that the tigers of Kheri had, for unknown reasons, begun "committing suicide."

"The sugar cane problem is unique to Dudhwa," Billy warned, "but the real clash is coming. When this place became a park, there were twenty-one villages on the outskirts; now there are eighty. Population is out of control everywhere in India, and the problem will spread as more and more tigers grow familiar with the humans encroaching on their territory and come to see them as prey. Familiarity breeds contempt."

Anything that moves is a target of opportunity for a tiger; their primary prey is deer, but when hungry enough they have been known to feed eagerly on anything from baby elephants to frogs and locusts—and instinct teaches them to sample whatever they kill. A herdsman killed trying to stop an attack on his buffalo at the park's edge may become a substitute for that buffalo. The next time, another herdsman may become the primary target.

Man-eaters, Jim Corbett argued, were simply animals which through "stress of circumstances" (wounds or old age) had been rendered incapable of pursuing their natural prey. Another circumstance helping to produce that fatal stress has traditionally been the steady degradation of the tiger's habitat and the prey species on which it normally depends. In order to survive in a steadily shrinking forest, some old or ailing tigers turned first to livestock and then to humans.

But during the 1980s, a third, still more troubling variety of man-eater began to emerge, and the brand new "stress of circumstance" that helped produce it was the success of the parks themselves as breeding grounds. Tigers are territorial animals. Although they sometimes cover twenty-four miles in a single night in search of food, the jungles through which they move are divided by them into a complex network of territories, their limits marked in a variety of ways—warning roars, scats, scratch marks on the ground, the meticulous spraying of trees and other natural boundary signs with scent.

The barriers between animals are not impenetrable: a tigress will sometimes share her territory with her grown daughters, and a resident male routinely allows several breeding females to occupy segments of his range. But he rarely shows similar generosity toward other males, and so, as tigers continued to breed within the undisturbed core areas, younger animals—or weakened older ones—were driven out toward the periphery in hopes of carving out new territories of their own. The forest corridors between parks which the planners of Project Tiger had hoped to maintain for just such migrants failed to materialize under the competing pressures of population and agriculture. These hungry, displaced animals have nowhere to go and are forced to cling to the forest edge, where natural prey is scarce and intrusions by human beings with their livestock increasingly common. Confrontations seemed inevitable.

They had already begun at Chitwan in Nepal, where, until 1980, there had been no documented cases of man-eating at all. Between 1980 and 1987, Charles McDougal told me, at least thirteen people were killed and eaten in and around that park, most of them by battered animals that had lost out in the fierce struggle for territory.

There is one region where generalizations about Indian man-eaters have never applied—the Sundarbans. There has not historically been any shortage of natural

prey in this huge forested delta, and the swampy terrain precludes permanent human habitation; yet tigers have systematically preyed upon people who have slipped up its canals and inlets by dugout to fish, cut wood, and collect wild honey at least since the seventeenth century. In 1666, François Bernier, a French traveler who visited the region, wrote that "among these islands, it is in many places dangerous to land, and great care must be had that the boat, which during the night is fastened to a tree, be kept at some distance from the shore, for it constantly happens that some person or another falls prey to tigers. These ferocious animals are very apt … to enter into the boat itself, while the people are asleep, and to carry away some victim, who, if we are to believe the boatmen of the country, generally happens to be the stoutest and fattest of the party."

It is still a dangerous place more than three centuries later. There are officially said to be some two hundred and fifty tigers in the Indian Sundarbans alone, the largest concentration anywhere on earth, and some—the experts disagree on how high a percentage—continue to be "opportunistic" man-eaters, ready to kill and eat any vulnerable human they happen to encounter. No one is certain why. Some believe that the daily tides that wash away the tigers' scent markings force the animals to be unusually aggressive in order to hold on to their territories. One study suggested that too much salt water might affect their livers, rendering them especially irritable, and sweet water ponds have been dug here and there in hopes of improving their equanimity—though why some tigers are driven to man-eating by salt water while others are not remains unexplained. Others argue that the seasonal flooding that makes life for the poor of neighboring Bangladesh so tenuous washes into the floating forest an annual harvest of corpses upon which scavenging tigers feed and thereby learn to associate human beings with food. (Jim Corbett believed that the man-eating leopards that suddenly emerged in the Kumaon Hills in his time had made the same deadly connection after feeding on abandoned victims of the influenza pandemic of 1917.)

In any case, the authorities urged villagers to wear clay masks on the back of their

Scavengers: Under the envious eye of a jackal, a jungle crow makes off with a gory morsel from a tiger's kill.

heads to confuse tigers (which are reluctant to attack their prey from the front). The annual number of killings in the Sundarbans was roughly halved, but recently, as honey-gatherers began to leave the uncomfortable masks at home, the death toll has begun to rise again.

Despite the continuing difficulties around the periphery of the Sundarbans, however, the great forest's inhospitability to man and the large number of tigers living within it relatively undisturbed make it the single most likely place for a permanent tiger population to persist.

"The tiger will survive in India," R. L. Singh once told me, "only so long as he behaves. The moment we try to be sentimental about any aberrant, defaulting tiger, the tiger will be doomed. Such tigers must be eliminated immediately to save innocent animals. Officers must act, not theorize. We are serving *people* first." He claims personally to have shot three man-eaters during his six years as park director at Dudhwa, and a total of ten animals was officially done away with. (Two more were captured and sent to the Lucknow Zoo, where they languished and died.) Billy himself was called upon to shoot several, a duty which for him was something akin to murder. "The fault is man's, of course," he said, "but the tigers are always made to pay."

Old-time professional hunters, forced to find other work after tiger shooting was banned, eagerly volunteered to oversee the culling of undesirable animals. "Despicable," Billy said. "They used to get ten thousand dollars a tiger from their clients before hunting was stopped. They just want to get back into the act." Their selflessness did seem suspect since they also wanted the right to contact rich overseas hunters and fly them in to do the shooting, a process that could have taken weeks while more innocent villagers died.

It is not easy to identify guilty tigers or to exonerate innocent ones. Those sent to execute man-eaters have no recourse but to fall back on the inexact science of identification by pug mark. Blameless animals have been killed, guilty ones allowed to continue their killing.

Some have suggested that "troublesome" tigers be transported to a forest where they are less likely to encounter humans. But other tigers often already occupy such places, and are less than hospitable to newcomers. Some years ago, a young Sundarbans tiger that had wandered out of the core area and killed first livestock and then a herdswoman was tranquilized, transported to a spot much deeper in the jungle and released. The resident male tiger killed it before the sun set.

Billy had not mellowed by the time I began to visit him, but he had matured. In the old days, battling single-handed to defend his park's borders, he had evinced little sympathy for the woodcutters and graziers and fishermen who dared encroach upon his tigers. He was still as vigilant as ever, but had begun to see that the poor were not the real enemy.

"How can you blame the cultivator?" he asks. "He has one acre of land and one bullock to plow it. If a tiger takes that bullock, what is he to do? No wonder he wants tigers done away with. It is *government's* fault. They have set up these parks and now they walk away from the problem.

"The local people hate the park," Billy told me as I drove off to talk with villagers in the surrounding countryside. "And they hate me. You'll see."

I left Tiger Haven along a twisting forest track, pausing twice, first to let a pair of

Pages 138–139:
The tigress Laxmi leads her brood across Ranthambhore's stony ground.

spotted deer spring across the road, and again to admire a huge crocodile sunning himself on the riverbank, then pulled onto the main road and almost immediately passed a wealthy sugar planter's concrete house surrounded by the thatched huts of his tenants. A gaudy wedding tent was set up in the landlord's garden with loudspeakers lashed to poles, so that his daughter's evening ceremony could be shared with his neighbors. A little further along, I stopped to let the groom's party pass, perhaps seventy-five laughing men in beards and turbans, dancing to the crash and blare of a brass band, on their way to the home of the bride.

Then I turned off onto an unpaved village road between green walls of sugar and stopped beside a field, where an old man was plowing behind a skeletal bullock. His name was Kanthulal, and he had lived here all his life. Things had been much better for him before the park was established, he said; in those days he had been able to collect his firewood without fear of arrest, could buy timber and thatch to shore up his house after the ravages of the monsoon. Hunters had kept the tigers down. Now he lived in fear. The wife of a boyhood friend had been killed cutting cane; he had himself twice seen tigers padding along the road and often spotted their fresh pug marks on his way to the fields in the early morning.

Two young cyclists stopped and walked their bicycles across the ruts to join us. They agreed with Kanthulal.

"We might as well be dogs, for all the interest government shows in us," one said, and the other nodded in vigorous agreement.

I continued on, past teams of cutters half hidden in the cane, and stopped beside the prosperous-looking young Sikh who was supervising their work. A tiger had recently slipped into his compound at night, he said, and had taken a fine buffalo. He had been helpless to do anything because he was not permitted a rifle. Forest officers had visited him but had done nothing either. The cane cutters echoed their foreman.

Billy was right: no one who lived around the park seemed to have a good word to say for it. Nor have most of the villagers who clustered in and around the other reserves I have visited ever seemed anything but resentful of the parks' existence, and it is hard to see why they should feel any differently. No one consulted them when the parks were carved out of forests they had always been more or less free to use. No one thought to compensate them adequately for their sacrifices.

Worse than that, in too many places and around too many parks, the laws barring their entry were flouted almost as soon as they were promulgated by forest personnel willing, even eager, to pocket bribes in exchange for letting livestock in and forest products out. To villagers without other sources of fuel and fodder, the government ban on entry seemed merely arbitrary, and the capriciousness with which it was applied further evidence of government's cynicism.

The villagers' view of the forests is ecologically shortsighted, of course. Most know only what their fathers knew—and the forest resources upon which their fathers unthinkingly relied have all but vanished. More than 300 million Indians have been born just since the birth of Project Tiger. And there may already be a billion head of livestock, almost all of it undernourished and forced to forage to survive.

"We face ecological disaster," the late Rajiv Gandhi once admitted, and with aid from abroad the central and state governments undertook massive reforestation projects. But trees continue to fall, precious grasslands are steadily devoured, whole hillsides tumble into rivers. You can see what is happening almost anywhere along the

Indian roads. Brightly painted trucks overloaded with new-cut logs careen around the curves. In the purple evening light, bands of barefoot women hurry home with heaps of branches balanced on their heads. Long lines of lean buffalo, gaunt cattle, scrawny goats drift out of the forest, leaving more acres stripped, and plod toward villages already shrouded in blue woodsmoke.

Until the government provides real benefits to the people whom the parks have displaced, Billy argued, "the only real answer that is fair to both sides is to keep people and tigers apart." He demanded a high electrified fence around Dudhwa to keep tigers in and people out, and a permanent ban on the growing of sugar cane within five miles of it.

But wouldn't that throw thousands of people off the land, I asked. Something else would have to be provided for them to do. Wasn't that too large an undertaking for a country with limited resources and so many pressing problems to assume?

"Saving the tiger—and the forests he lives in—is itself a large undertaking," Billy stubbornly responded. "If we are serious about it, we have no choice."

Conservation is always a question of priorities, and Billy's are clear: "Tigers need unmolested forest in which to multiply. People can breed anywhere."

One evening at the end of my first visit to Dudhwa, I sat with Billy across a stream from a kill made by the tigress he believed to be his Tara. The moon cast just enough light for us to make out her big silhouette, but we could clearly hear her muttering as she tore at her kill, alarming yet natural sounds that have been made here since the beginning of time.

Then, a new and ultimately more ominous noise drifted toward us from across the cane fields at our back: the amplified drone of the wedding priest in the nearby village, reading out verses from the Sikh holy book, the *Granth Sahib*. A new family was beginning; still more people would soon edge toward the tiger's last retreat.

It was already hard to hear the cracking of the bones.

## CHAPTER EIGHT
# BESIEGED

One afternoon during the winter of 1986 I was dozing in my room in the Jogi Mahal at Ranthambhore when I was awakened by a soft, silky sound. Standing at the end of my bed was a young, slender Indian woman, wearing a peacock blue sari and smiling down at me with what seemed like a lover's admiration. I thought I was dreaming until her husband, a squat little man with glasses, slipped in, and stood at her side, also beaming.

They were gazing at the bed, not at me, they explained; eager to have *darshan* (an auspicious view) of the place where Rajiv and Sonia Gandhi had slept just a few weeks earlier. The Gandhis' vacation visit to Ranthambhore—during which Fateh Singh Rathore's luck had held and a tiger stalked and killed a deer within yards of the jeep in which the prime minister sat—had set off a stampede of visitors. Suddenly, it was fashionable to go to Ranthambhore and see a tiger.

Despite Fateh's determined guardianship, Ranthambhore has always been a fragile place, under constant siege. Some threats to its survival were traditional. Nomadic hunters camped on the fringes just long enough to send packs of lean dogs coursing after small mammals for their skins. Untouchables poached an occasional chital in hopes of making a meager profit selling the meat in the market at Sawai Madhopur. Muslim townspeople sometimes slipped inside to shoot, too, because they like to serve deer on festive occasions.

But now, the park's newfound fame as the most likely place in India to see a tiger brought with it another threat whose long-term impact was not yet fully understood. The tigers and other animals remained largely oblivious to solitary vehicles, but the number of these clamorous intruders increased almost overnight. Long lines of jeeps and Land Rovers now whined through the forest, morning and evening, scattering the herds of deer as their eager passengers leaned out to shout at one another, "Have you seen the tiger? Have you seen the tiger?"

Fateh had drawn up stringent rules for visitors, but the staff was always too small to ensure that they were followed: once a tiger was spotted, for example, no more than three vehicles were ever supposed to congregate at the site; but in practice, word of a tiger spread instantly and within minutes a dozen jeeps and Land Rovers roared toward the spot, shrouding the roads in dust, filling the forest with the acrid smell of diesel fuel.

Similar things happened at all the most accessible reserves. Every morning at Kanha, elephants and their mahouts scoured the jungle for a tiger on its kill, and when one was found, staged what they called a "Tiger Show," ferrying tourists to and from the site by elephant to take pictures. So many eager visitors lined up to climb aboard that ladders for mounting were placed at strategic points along the forest roads and numbered brass checks had to be handed out just to keep the queues orderly.

I attended one "Tiger Show," crowding with three other people onto a swaying elephant that shouldered its way between two others until we were within four yards of a bamboo thicket in which a big tiger lay on top of its kill. A quartet of wealthy

*Opposite:* A tiger finds sanctuary at Bandhavgarh.

Indian women, clutching their purses and wearing bright saris, occupied the elephant to my right. Although the tiger was no further than ten feet from them, they could not seem to see it through the leaves.

"Where is it?" one called out.

"I can't see it either," answered her companion, reaching out to part the bamboo and leaning down. "Ah, *there* it is!"

Her face was within eight feet of the tiger's. Crouched over its spotted deer, it kept up a low, steady rumble of annoyance as she clicked away with the camera dangling from her neck. After what seemed a very long five minutes, we turned and lumbered back to the road so that more elephant-loads of tourists could be brought in for a close-up look.

All someone had to do to bring about a tragedy was drop a camera or a purse—or simply lean too far and slide off the elephant. And, I was told, the mahouts, whose tips rose the closer they could get their passengers to their quarry, sometimes upped the odds still further. One was relieved of his duties at another park after he was found prodding a tiger with a long stick to make it snarl for an especially zealous foreign photographer.

Worse than even the most heedless tourists are the ubiquitous VIPs—politicians and government officials, accompanied by cronies, servants, securitymen, and family members—who descend upon the parks in good weather as if they were their private fiefdoms and the park directors and forest staffs their body servants. VIPs commandeer rest houses, monopolize elephants and vehicles and guides, and too often see no need to obey any of the rules ordinary citizens are expected to follow. At Ranthambhore one afternoon, Valmik and I watched helplessly as an Indian Air Force general ordered his terrified chauffeur to drive his official jeep again and again into a clump of bushes in order to force the badly injured tigress sheltering there out into the open so that he could snap a picture of her. The tigress did finally burst from the thicket, one bloody paw held in the air, and lurched off as best she could on her three good legs. The general cursed his driver for failing to provide him with the proper angle.

Even tourism might have been controlled in time. The park's ultimate fate really rested in the hands of the 225,000 villagers, mostly members of the Meena tribe, who still lived on its periphery with some 150,000 head of hungry livestock.

Like virtually all of India's parks and sanctuaries, Ranthambhore had become an island in a sea of people by the late 1980s. Under the relentless pressure of population, the adjacent forests and grasslands in which young tigers were meant to disperse had virtually disappeared, hacked down for firewood and chewed up by the big herds of scrawny goats, cows, and buffalo which wandered through them daily in search of what little greenery might have escaped them the day before.

To the herdsmen who live around it, the thickets and meadows of Ranthambhore represent the most convenient source of fuel and fodder otherwise unavailable to them, and the result has been a more or less constant state of border war between them and the small force of forest guards with orders to keep them out.

Fateh remained determined to defend his ramparts, but he also knew that in the long run, mere militancy would never work. The villages grew every year; so did their dependence upon the forest. Unless their needs could be changed or met some other way, unless the villagers could be made to see that the park's survival was of some direct benefit to them, it was doomed.

In 1985, he and Valmik Thapar drew up an ambitious five-year action plan: local banks agreed to provide low-interest loans with which to purchase improved livestock for those villagers willing to stay out of the forest, for example, and the Forest Department itself would feed those new cattle on grass grown exclusively for that purpose on forest lands outside the park. Mobile educational units were to move from village to village, explaining the principles of conservation, warning of what would happen to human as well as animal life if the forests were finished off.

"We proposed that such measures be put on a war footing," Thapar remembers. "But it was one thing to draw up a plan. Implementation was something else. Nothing was done, government priorities clashed, and things got worse. Tigers don't vote, so local politicians supported grazing. Then the rains stopped."

Left alone, nature had restored Ranthambhore. Now, in uneasy collaboration with man, it threatened to destroy it. Three consecutive years of drought, the worst in this century, seared Rajasthan, shrinking Ranthambhore's famous lakes to shallow pools ringed by dried mud, and withering what little fodder the already parched countryside that surrounds the park might have offered to the villagers who lived there.

The rains would come again, of course. They always do eventually. The lakes would fill up again and the forest would recover fully if left alone. But the ever-growing numbers of people who lived outside the park couldn't wait for nature to take its leisurely course. Ranthambhore's grass and timber now seemed their last defense against disaster, and they poured across its borders in greater numbers than ever before.

After three years of bitter, worsening strife with villagers and the Forest Department, the District Collector in 1987 bowed to pressure from desperate herdsmen and granted permission for them to take their hungry herds into the park. Thousands of cattle swarmed through Ranthambhore's ravines. Powerless either to keep them out or to protect the herdsmen from possible attack by his tigers, Fateh Singh resigned his post. It took the personal intervention of Rajiv Gandhi to have the collector disciplined, the herdsmen driven out again, and Fateh restored to power. But he had become the focus of so much controversy by then that he was finally ordered to take up new duties elsewhere.

Fateh Singh Rathore.

He refused to go. "How can I leave this place after twenty years?" he asked. "It has been my life. Whatever happens, I am here. I will never go away." He had built himself a farmhouse on the western edge of the park and planned to live on there for the rest of his life, driving into the park every day to do what he could on his own to keep Ranthambhore alive.

"We do the best we can," Fateh's successor told me. "But it is very difficult. The graziers used to come in small groups, no more than fifteen men at a time. One or two forest guards could take care of them. Now they come in hundreds, sometimes thousands."

On a single summer day that same year, three thousand herdsmen led fifteen thousand hungry cattle into Ranthambhore's ravines. It took an army of policemen, home guards, and agents of the Revenue Department and a pitched battle during which shots were fired to help the Forest Department drive them out again. The graziers and woodcutters were back the next day, and the next.

Several months later, while visiting Fateh at home, I asked if he'd take me on a long drive—first along the park's borders, so that I could see for myself how the forest fared without protection, then inside, following roads most visitors never saw.

We sped past mile after mile of stony hillside, broken only by dusty stumps and long since emptied of all but the most tenacious wildlife. Fateh stopped to point out the spot where the previous year he had found three dead tiger cubs, their bodies emaciated, their skulls crushed by their mother, evidently unable to find enough natural prey to feed herself, let alone her growing offspring. He buried the cubs beneath the great banyan tree behind Jogi Mahal.

Despite the memory, Fateh's fierce, natural optimism seemed intact. As we started off again, he spoke of the "beautiful" root stock still stubbornly alive beneath the seared slopes. "All this needs is a little protection and it can be a fantastic forest again," he told me, and scattered patches of green hillside, which he had managed imperfectly to shelter with barbed wire for just a few seasons, seemed to prove him right: even the most degraded forest can come back if given enough unmolested time.

But there was no time. We entered the park through an entrance rarely used by visitors. Fateh hadn't been in this area for weeks, and was braced to see some damage, but he was clearly not ready for the devastation that was suddenly everywhere around us.

"It's a massacre," he said. Whole trees lay across the track, leaves still bright green, felled just that morning by spiteful graziers to demonstrate to the Forest Department its powerlessness to stop them. A little further along, six men hurried off the road and into a gully at our clamorous approach, balancing great bundles of freshly cut grass on their heads as they ran. Broad expanses of tall, sun-bleached grass, remembered from earlier visits, had been cropped to stubble. The half-dried droppings of cattle were scattered everywhere, big as dinner plates. And on the road were camel and tractor tracks, signs that vehicles filled with wood were regularly being hauled from the heart of the core area with the apparent connivance of members of the forest staff.

"Twenty years of work ... gone, like that," Fateh raised one hand from the wheel in a rare, helpless gesture. "Two, three more years of this and it will all be finished." He lapsed into uncharacteristic silence, punctuated now and again by a soft "Oof," as we passed yet another despoiled thicket, another chewed-over clearing.

Toward midday we followed a twisting, deeply rutted road that led up a long slope to the highest point in the park, and stopped on the summit near a cairn of stones on which Fateh used to like to stand and survey the sprawling forest to which he had devoted most of his adult life.

"I haven't been to the cinema hall in twenty-five years," he said. "This is my cinema."

From here, Ranthambhore seemed at first as it had always been, the violet hills stretching away in all directions, the rutting calls of chital stags echoing across the slopes beneath a sky of unbroken blue. But as I peered more closely, I could see that some of the dark shapes browsing in the grassy clearings below were domestic buffalo, not deer; the tops of the outermost hills were strangely saw-toothed, the undergrowth already eaten away, leaving only the tallest trees standing; and broad patches of the hillsides themselves had been stripped bare.

The Ranthambhore forest was visibly retreating, its buffer zone already largely a thing of the past. A fourth scorching summer was soon to come. The herds would grow more voracious, their owners more desperate. And there was still no certainty of rain.

Back at Fateh's farm on the park's edge that evening, the desert air was still cold and we huddled around a fire. Despite a strong drink and the brilliant display of stars, our host was unusually quiet, still dispirited by the damage we'd seen in our day-long drive.

Why did he stay on here, I asked him. How could he stand by and see the forest for which he very nearly sacrificed his life eaten away, day after day, and be unable to do anything to stop it?

He continued to stare into the flames. "I am an Indian," he said finally. "If I die, I die, but we must not let this place die. Ranthambhore is like the Taj Mahal. It belongs to us and to our children and grandchildren. I can never leave it."

As he spoke, I grew gradually aware of what seemed at first to be the rasping sound of sawing wood, coming from somewhere in the plundered forest behind me.

Fateh brightened, held up his hand: "That's a leopard."

He jumped up from his chair, strode out of the circle of firelight, and, legs spread wide and head thrown back, snarled into the darkness.

The leopard answered him, and as we listened, Fateh Singh Rathore and the unseen cat continued to call to one another through the Rajasthan night.

Clearly, the old antagonistic relationship between the parks' guardians and those they guarded them against was not working, at Ranthambhore or anywhere else in India.

H. S. Panwar, former field director at Kanha and ex-director of Project Tiger, was among the earliest advocates of working out some new kind of rapprochement between parks and people before it is too late. He is a small, voluble, resolute man who now heads the Wildlife Institute of India at Dehra Dun, training Forest Department officials in wildlife management and awarding advanced degrees in biology.

We've often run across its eager young degree candidates in our travels: fearlessly collecting the viscera from fresh tiger and leopard kills in order to study the diet of chital and nilghai at Sariska; sitting motionless in a tree for hours each day to observe the mating rituals of the endangered Bengal florican at Dudhwa; providing an omniscient escort for an expert from the U.S. Fish and Wildlife Service conducting an all-Indian survey of raptors. Their elders understandably give in to weary pessimism about the future of Indian wildlife from time to time; these enthusiastic young people, at least, seem committed to seeing that it has one.

"A new relationship with the people in and around the parks is desperately needed," Panwar told me, "but it's not easy to achieve." Rajaji National Park, just a few miles from Dehra Dun, provides a good example. It is filled with the camps of some five thousand graziers—*gujjars*—and their ten thousand buffalo. In the old days, the herdsmen and their livestock spent from October to February there, then moved up into the mountains to summer their herds in alpine pastures during the monsoon. That way, the fodder in both places was given time to recover each year. But the herds have grown so large that the hill people have barred their pastures to them, and most *gujjars* now simply stay year-round in the valley, where their animals are methodically devouring the forest while leaving untouched twisted thickets of lantana and other unpalatable plants of no use to wildlife.

The result—under the nose of the Wildlife Institute, within a few miles of the headquarters of the state Forest Department—is a steadily accelerating disaster. The trees

*Pages 148–149:*
The tiger that researchers called Kublai, stalking its prey at Ranthambhore.

on the crests of the hills have already been lopped for firewood, so that the summer sun pours in to desiccate the forest floor. Monsoon rains wash the loosened soil down the slopes, widening the riverbeds, causing flash floods, doing still further damage to the already dwindling forest.

An effort was recently made to provide the *gujjars* with alternative housing outside the park. No one bothered to consult the herdsmen themselves as to their needs. Instead, hundreds of thousands of rupees were spent building cement structures utterly unlike anything the *gujjars* had ever known before and providing too little room for the animals that are their livelihood. Understandably enough, they refused to move. A local politician took up their cause.

The *gujjars* remain. The cement city stands empty. Buffalo are everywhere. Rajaji is disappearing.

"We can no longer look to government for all the answers," Panwar said. "Delhi is too far away. State governments are rarely interested. There are too many problems, too many conflicting demands, for the proper focus on wildlife to be maintained."

At first, an enlightened central government had seemed Indian conservation's brightest hope. Indian politics are intensely personalized, and in large part because Jawaharlal Nehru, his daughter Indira Gandhi, and his grandson Rajiv all took a personal interest in wildlife, New Delhi has traditionally shown concern for its preservation. But now that assassination has removed the Nehru-Gandhi family from the political scene, at least for the foreseeable future, the enthusiasm of its successors, confronted with so many other pressing problems, has yet to show itself.

Meanwhile, day-to-day care of the sanctuaries remains with the states, where clashing priorities undercut even the most carefully drawn-up plans and too many officials see the forests simply as a means to personal gain: the going rate for a cycle-load of wood illegally cut in Rajaji was said to be fifteen rupees when I visited there, for example, and hundreds of thousands of cycle-loads were being taken out each year. Similar raids on park resources are routinely undertaken all across the country. The especially able director of one park in Madhya Pradesh is said to have been removed from his job when he dared prosecute a powerful local landowner for setting up a weekend hunting camp in the heart of his preserve; he ended up guarding a timber depot far from the forests he loved. S. Deb Roy, the former field director of the Manas Tiger Reserve in Assam and one of the ablest and most dedicated of all of India's Tiger-Wallahs, was summarily removed from the top wildlife post of his state when he refused to go along with a cabal of local politicians determined to continue illegally felling the already shrinking state forests. "Wildlife management is a thankless task," he once told me. "There is no money in it for an honest man. When I retire I will not even have enough money saved to buy a house or educate my children. The rewards are only personal. You must love wildlife for itself."(Deb Roy continues to love it for itself, fighting on from Delhi though he is no longer in government.)

"It is not enough to declare forests sanctuaries but fail to do anything for the people we displace," Panwar continued. "Unless we provide the people with alternate sources of fuel and fodder, how can they help but hate us? Wildlife management used to be eighty percent enforcement, twenty percent management. That doesn't work any more. Something else is needed. We must somehow include the people, or they will overthrow us."

Vallmik Thapar had come to the same conclusion all on his own, and late one winter afternoon in 1987 I sat with him on the flat roof of a small house he had just built for himself on the western edge of the park. The setting sun bathed the stony, treeless hills in front of us with gold, and in that burnished light a regal procession moved slowly along the only road—scores of women in red and orange saris going home, each balancing on her head a bundle of grass longer than she was tall, in a line that stretched half a kilometer. Behind them, scores of buffalo and cattle and goats, their bellies filled with precious grass and foliage, also plodded toward home. The musical *tunk* of wooden cowbells echoed across the fields. A visitor could not help but admire the beauty of it.

"It is beautiful. Who can deny it?" Valmik said. "But the park is literally being eaten up, and there are far too many to stop. These people are not simply going to go away."

When I first knew Valmik, his interests had not extended much beyond the jungle where he preferred to spend all but the hottest hours of every day, observing his tigers. Villagers were intruders, to be driven out.

But he had changed over the years, had come to see—as Fateh privately had, too—that the Indian conservation movement had to change as well, if there was to be any hope of the forests' survival, and that it would do no good to wait for the state or the Center to act. India's wildlife could only be saved by India's citizens. And so, in 1987—the second year of the drought that withered Ranthambhore, the year Fateh was removed from his post—this big but retiring man from New Delhi who had found his real home in the heart of the jungle, had now virtually abandoned it. Instead, he had taken it upon himself to launch the Ranthambhore Foundation, a non-profit, non-governmental organization whose goal was somehow to transform the villagers who were ravaging the park into its protectors.

"Why should we blame these people for being shortsighted?" he asked. "They're not stupid. They've been living here since long before we city dwellers got interested in this place. Yet no one asked them whether there should be a park here. No one warned them that entering the park to graze their herds or gather firewood as they always had would suddenly make them criminals. They're right that the park does not benefit them, at least not in the short run. It's our job to change that, to help them see that their survival and that of the park are linked, that if the forest is destroyed, their lives and all our lives will be destroyed, as well."

It was and is a dismaying task. Villagers are traditionally wary of change, and still more suspicious of citified outsiders. Valmik began by buying several acres of stony, degraded land, dug a well, built himself the simple house atop which we sat and planted trees around it. Otherwise, he planned to leave the landscape alone, trusting it to revive on its own and demonstrate to the nearby villagers how quickly the forest could grow again.

As the sun set, he excitedly outlined for me the ambitious plans he had drawn up with the advice of friends from Delhi and abroad: a mobile van to provide primary health care while spreading the word about the importance of preserving forests; a crafts program for women to earn extra money for their families; a dairy cooperative and the introduction of better breeds of cows and buffalo to demonstrate the advantages of stall-fed animals that thrive—and yield far more milk—without ever having to enter the forest; programs to persuade people to plant trees and introduce children to the beauty of the forest before it vanished.

Pilgrims at the annual Ganesh festival at Ranthambhore trying to get home: Hundreds of thousands of the faithful make their way to and from an ancient temple within the park each year, disturbing wildlife and disrupting management.

The foundation planned to extend its activities to just a few villages on the fringe of Ranthambhore. Ranthambhore itself was just one park, its famous tigers and the hooved prey on which they fed constituted only a tiny fraction of India's wildlife legacy. Still, if Ranthambhore could somehow be saved despite all the problems that surrounded it, it would demonstrate at least that survival was possible. "If it can be done here," Valmik told me, "it can be done anywhere." He seemed tireless and hopeful, but also cautious about the future. "Let's see," he said. "It's only a beginning."

To a visitor, it all seemed exciting—at last someone was doing something—but it was also hard to see how it could succeed. The task was too big, Ranthambhore's problems too great. And, surrounded by acres of despoiled, still-treeless landscape, Valmik's new house seemed very small.

Although man-eating continued at Dudhwa, and so did the random revenge killing of tigers, the Forest Department continued to allow human intrusions into the park. Over Billy's vehement objections, licenses were still routinely issued for the removal of dead wood and other forest products, and those who gathered them were still allowed to risk their lives on the tigers' territory.

"Mixed use doesn't work," Billy kept saying, "at least it doesn't work here." Driving through the park one winter day in 1987, I had a vivid glimpse of what he meant. A bullock cart creaked toward us along the forest road, bearing a huge, gnarled tree trunk. Not a hundred feet behind it stalked a big male tiger, belly nearly to the ground, his stare so fixed upon his intended target that at first he did not see our vehicle. Whether it was the bullocks that had caught his eye, or the oblivious old man who drove them, we will never know, for our presence spoiled the tiger's stalk: he finally stopped, glared at us, glared at his retreating prey, then turned off into the forest.

Finally, fearful that if such incursions weren't ended there would be still more man-eating and the tiger-poisoning that inevitably follows it, Billy went to the high court and obtained a stay order against the Forest Department, invoking the Indian Wildlife Act of 1972 to bar all further wood gathering within the park. Billy's court order may well have come too late. The human tide continued steadily to rise. In 1968, there were already twenty-one villages on the periphery of the park; there were now more than eighty, and more are likely to spring up. Yet there was still no provision for providing the villagers with alternative fuel. A politician won a state assembly seat by promising to reopen the forest to all comers.

There had always been more or less constant nighttime poaching around the park—difficult to detect because farmers use firecrackers to drive the deer and wild boar from the cane fields. But during that same visit I heard for the first time of jeeploads of drunken policemen and wealthy farmers driving through the park after dark, shooting whatever they liked, and of organized gangs of poachers shipping tiger skins to Nepal.

The rate of confrontation between man and tiger had declined, though, as Billy says, whether it was because of his ban or simply that tiger numbers had plummeted, no one can be sure.

Whether or not his ban saved lives, it was evidently the last straw for the Forest Department, which found itself deprived of the revenue that had been generated by the luctative harvesting of wood—licit and illicit. It seemed only a matter of time before someone would find a way to strike back against the seventy-one-year-old man who had created the park it now managed, and who insisted that it become in fact what it had been intended to be on paper—a genuine sanctuary for the last surviving remnant of *terai* wildlife.

Billy Arjan Singh strides through the Dudhwa jungle.

The retaliation was brutal when it came. On December 17, 1988, a canter filled with armed forest guards clanked onto Billy's property. They pushed their way onto the verandah, cursed the servants and Billy's sister-in-law, seized a heap of firewood, ripped down the lights Billy had used to illuminate his baited kills, and smashed the bridge the Forest Department itself had built over the Soheli to join Tiger Haven with the park.

Billy looked on in shock, helpless. "What have I done?" he kept asking. "What have I done?" Three young students from the Wildlife Institute happened to be visiting when the invasion arrived. They broke into tears. As the destruction continued, one fell to his knees and kissed Billy's hands.

Billy was formally charged with stealing wood from the forest, of all things (bureaucrats have their own heavy-handed sense of irony)—and with baiting in defiance of Project Tiger rules in order to entertain the handful of tourists who visit the farm each year. (Billy's baiting was not in fact being done for tourists—as a good many disappointed visitors to Tiger Haven can attest—but in order, first, to keep track of the tigress he believed to be Tara, and, after she finally disappeared, to provide sustenance to a big male which Billy feared might otherwise become a man-eater, because its canine teeth had been blown out by a bomb and it could no longer open its own kills.)

Still worse, Billy was formally barred from his park and then made subject to more or less continuous official harassment, to which Diane and I were once witnesses.

It was shortly after noon on a crisp winter's morning several weeks after the Forest Department raid, and warm enough at last so that we were enjoying our ice-cold

Since no alternative sources of fodder or firewood have ever been made available to them, women living in the villages that surround Sariska have little choice but to defy the law, enter the park, and ravage what little remains of its forest.

shandies—tumblers of beer and lemonade—before lunch was served. Before us, beyond the big tree that shades the whitewashed house, open fields stretched on toward the solid green wall of sugar cane that forms the horizon.

There were five of us on the verandah. Diane and I, Balram and Mira, and Billy, wearing a T-shirt and shorts that still revealed massive biceps and thighs like tree trunks. The memory of the forest raid was painfully raw and one could sense Billy's embarrassment at being unable even to enter the park; but the talk for the moment was of boxing, about which Billy and his brother are omniscient, though unable to see any bouts unless some foreign visitor remembers to bring along a videocassette. The newspapers had come from Calcutta only a few days late, and we were lazily discussing Mike Tyson's prospects against his next opponent.

A troupe of the drab, raucous gray birds called the Seven Sisters hopped about the verandah in search of crumbs left behind after yesterday's tea.

A crow lit on the roof and began a desultory cawing.

Then we heard a crashing sound.

Billy hurled his newspaper to the ground, was up and out of his chair and plunging across the field, thick legs pumping, fists balled, before any of the rest of us could speak. His tracker, Suresh, was right behind him.

The rest of us stumbled off the porch to watch.

An elephant had emerged from the forest onto Billy's land. Three men sat on its back: a mahout and two men in khaki, one of whom was very fat and holding upright an ancient shotgun. He wore a cap with ear flaps and brightly polished shoes.

The elephant eyed Billy as he continued to storm toward her, and began to flap her ears.

He was shouting now: "Get off my land! Get off my land!"

"We have our orders," said the man with the gun. He and his companion were with the Forest Department. The fat man was the park's deputy director. "We are checking to see if you are baiting for tigers."

"I will do what I want on my own land! " Billy said. He stood within six feet of the elephant now, and shook his big fist. "I can *bury* you on my land."

The elephant was getting nervous, and as she shifted her feet, the fat man didn't seem to know just what to do with his gun. His shiny shoes hung out over the elephant's sides. His hat slipped down over one eye.

"We have our orders," he said finally. The gun waved in the air.

"Come down from that elephant," Billy said, "and I'll break your face."

The elephant was rocking back and forth now. She wanted to go home, to get away from this angry, gesticulating man. So did her riders. The elephant broke into a clumsy trot back toward the forest. The fat man gripped the howdah with one hand to keep from falling off, the shotgun wavering dangerously in the other.

Billy stalked after them for a few yards, still shaking his fist, then started back toward his house for lunch. He seemed enormously cheered and ten years younger.

How could he bear it, I asked Billy after lunch. Asked the same question, Fateh had said that to surrender would be to betray his country. Not Billy. "India is a dying animal," he said, "with all the vultures descending to see what they can get out of the carcass. If the animals left the forest, I couldn't stomach it here. I'd leave this bloody country."

What was it, then, that made him keep fighting? "A quirk of personality," he said, eyes flashing with something of their old fire. "I could not live with myself if I gave up. The tigers would have no advocate, no voice."

In 1989, Fateh finally wearied of sitting on the sidelines at Ranthambhore and agreed to accept appointment as field director at Sariska, the tiger reserve where I had done my boyhood hunting and where he had once been stationed as a lowly ranger. I visited him there not long after he took over, and one afternoon, as we slammed our way up a scrub-covered hillside, the angry, staccato coughs of langurs volleyed back and forth across the park's long, narrow valley. They had clearly spotted a predator on the prowl. Fateh sat in the back of the open Land Rover, urging the driver on. "Quickly, quickly, quickly," he muttered, as we ground around a curve.

The Land Rover jerked to a stop. On the slope just above us, a big leopard crouched behind the chital he had just killed. Paws crossed neatly on his prey's white belly, he panted from exertion and glared at us, his muzzle smeared with blood. We were not the only witnesses. Perhaps twenty feet from the kill stood a sambar hind with her small offspring. Head down, her gaze fixed on the big cat, she belled steadily—a sound not unlike a truck horn—and advanced gingerly toward him, tail up, front hoof stomping loudly. The leopard looked at us, looked at the indignant deer, finally got up and slipped into the nearest thicket where, although he now lay no more than thirty feet from us, he was instantly invisible. The hind continued to inch toward him—two or three stomping steps, a pause, then a loud *bonk*, then the stomping again. It went on for fifteen minutes before the hungry leopard had had enough. He rose to his feet and snarled. The sambar came to her senses and crashed away through the undergrowth.

Night was falling now, and as we drove back to Fateh's quarters, wrapping ourselves tightly against the sudden desert cold, I found myself babbling about how handsome the leopard had been, how lucky we had been to see him so clearly.

*Pages 156–157:*
In the evening, a tigress stalks below the sprawling Ranthambhore fortress.

Fateh was uncharacteristically silent. He agreed finally that leopards were handsome, but explained that the smaller predator's bold presence in broad daylight was just further evidence of the sad fate of the tigers the park was meant to protect. If tigers were present in sufficient numbers in the heart of the park, he explained, gingerly leopards would keep to its periphery.

As recently as 1988, there were officially said to be forty-five resident tigers, although that figure was very likely inflated by Fateh's predecessor. In any case, he explained, there were now no more than sixteen. The rest had been shot. Eighteen tigers and thirty or more leopards were believed to have been killed in and around the park over the six years before Fateh took up his new post. A local tribesman confessed to having done the actual shooting with an ancient muzzleloader, but he was said to have been aided and abetted by nearby villagers eager to ensure the safety of their sheep and goats and cattle, by poorly paid Forest Department personnel just as eager for a share of the profits, and by a big-time smuggler who lived in Old Delhi.

Poaching is common in India, and punishment of poachers all too rare. There are rarely witnesses. Forest and police officials are sometimes themselves involved and often prefer to look the other way. A single celebrated poacher named Veerappan is said to have accounted for more than three hundred elephants along the border between Karnataka and Tamil Nadu—and to have cut and sold off thousands of acres of protected sandalwood into the bargain—while the police and forest departments of two states have proved unable to track him down. When one courageous forest officer dared try to trap him, Veerappan had him dismembered as an example to others who might be tempted to try the same thing.

Sariska is a deceptive place. On paper, it sprawls over 800 square kilometers, and anyone driving through in the evening who sees the herds of deer that line the tarred road that runs through its heart is easily convinced that it must be one of India's richest parks—as I was upon my return to India in 1983. In reality, only a strip of valley twenty kilometers long and two kilometers wide turns out ever to have received genuine protection—and even here I've seen grasscutters scurrying to safety, dropping their bright green bundles as they run—and the thick herds of deer along the road have been lured there to please tourists by a system of artificial water holes.

Fateh showed me that back from the main road, out of sight of most visitors, the slopes were largely barren of animal life. We drove for a time along a low stone wall that divides protected acres of wild platinum-colored grass blowing gently in the breeze from the grassless, stony ground outside, where cattle continued to graze unchecked. There was a break in the wall, and Fateh bellowed to a forest guard to shoo a cow back outside. The cow heaved herself over the stones and trotted for a few yards before stopping to wait for us to leave.

We climbed the wooded hillside, grateful for the dappled shade, then lurched onto the summit. The sun was suddenly blinding. There were five villages scattered across the broad plateau, low clusters of graziers' huts circled by crude walls woven of thorn bushes. Otherwise, there was nothing but treeless, grassless, chewed-over wasteland. A herdboy, balanced on a stick and one leg, watched us pass. The three wasted buffalo under his care did not even look up, continuing to nose their way over the parched ground in search of some surviving scrap to eat.

A lone nilghai antelope clattered off across the desert of fist-sized stones.

Unless things improved, the whole park would one day look like this—and like the ravaged featureless land that stretches in every direction beyond its borders.

Fateh had done his best to reverse things. The traffic that once honked its way down the valley had largely been diverted, and worship at a temple sacred to the monkey-god Hanuman that used to bring hundreds of pilgrims into the park each evening was limited to one day a week. He built new roads for patrolling, diverted watercourses to spread precious water more equally through the parched forest so that where there had been no animals when he took charge, there were now scattered bands of sambar and nilghai. We saw the tracks of a tigress and three cubs and the spot where they had sat together and played during the night, the dust still holding the faint marks of their twitching tails. And we saw where the pug marks of a big male had crossed theirs, as well.

"We must have the time to change things." Fateh snapped his fingers. "You cannot do it like *that*."

Fateh was not finally permitted to do it at all. The odds against him quickly proved too great. Scores of villages ring the park, their inhabitants enviously eyeing its grass and wood. His staff was small, poorly paid, unarmed. He managed to cajole the residents of at least one village to move out of the park to a site just beyond its borders, only to find the state and central governments reluctant to come up with the funds with which to relocate them. There were threats to kill him from herdsmen he had barred from the park, and from mining interests whose licenses to pillage roughly one fifth of it, obtained largely through the wholesale purchase of politicans, he had sought to have canceled in court.

In the end, Fateh had made too many enemies. Mine owners organized demonstrations against him. And his superiors in the Forest Department, weary of the trouble that seemed to follow him everywhere, angered by his lack of tact, his unwillingness to be silent when poaching took place, and his refusal to compromise when he felt the good of his park was at stake—and perhaps envious as well of the celebrity his photographs and books and foreign friends had brought him—removed him from Sariska. Then, using as a pretext a court case contesting his right to the land on which his farm stands, they suspended him from the department. He went home to Ranthambhore.

By 1990, both Billy and Fateh found themselves barred from the parks to which they had devoted their lives. Meanwhile, reports were beginning to filter in from everywhere that Project Tiger was in trouble, that the tigers' fortunes might have fatally been reversed.

## CHAPTER NINE

# MASSACRE

I n late June 1992 I received a letter and a set of newspaper clippings from Fateh. Several poachers had been arrested at Ranthambhore; they had confessed to the police that they had shot more than fifteen tigers there over the past two years. And they were not alone. Several other poaching gangs, they said, were at work in and around the park.

Rumors of tiger poaching had swirled around Ranthambhore since 1990, but the Chief Wildlife Warden of the state had dismissed them all as "baseless," the products of "vested interests" (by which he seems mostly to have meant Fateh, without a job again and noisily unhappy at what was happening to the sanctuary he still considered his). Some 31,000 tourists, more than half of them foreigners, visited the park during the winter of 1990–91, an all-time record, and a good many complained that they had seen no signs of tigers, let alone the tigers themselves. Noon—the tigress that had mastered the technique of killing in the lakes, the animal I had watched feeding with her cubs in the grass two years earlier—seemed suddenly to be missing. So was the magnificent tiger called the Bokhala male. So were other individual animals well known to Fateh and Valmik and to the guides and jeep drivers who made locating tigers their business.

A story about the mysterious dearth of tiger sightings at Ranthambhore appeared in the *Indian Express* in February 1992. The field director claimed there was nothing to worry about: because of an unusually heavy monsoon the previous summer, the tigers were simply keeping to the hills. In March, the erstwhile Maharani of Jaipur, whose hunting reserve Ranthambhore once had been, also expressed her concern. She, too, was told nothing was wrong, and when the census was taken that summer, sure enough, the official total was forty-five tigers, one more than had been claimed the year before.

Fateh made more trouble for himself by publicly denouncing its accuracy: If there were that many tigers, why weren't they being seen? He was sure there weren't more than twenty tigers left in the park.

The rumors persisted. During our visit to Ranthambhore that winter, the corpse of Badhiya, a forest guard who had been one of the most knowledgeable and dedicated members of the forest staff, was found sprawled along the railroad tracks outside the park. There were whispers he'd been murdered because he knew too much about poaching.

Something was very wrong. Even the Forest Department began to worry, and when the census was undertaken the following May, Valmik Thapar was asked to help conduct it. The results were devastating: he could find concrete evidence of only seventeen tigers in the park, and tentative evidence suggesting there might be three more. Again, the Chief Wildlife Warden denied everything. The census was faulty, he insisted, botched by the same amateurs he himself had asked for help.

But then came the arrests. Gopal Moghiya, a member of a traditional hunting tribe who ordinarily worked as watchmen for local herdsmen, was seized by the

*Opposite:* Noon rests on a rock shelf overlooking a water hole; one of the most trusting of Ranthambhore's tigers, she is believed to have been one of the first to have been slaughtered by poachers.

Sawai Madhopur Police, along with the skin and bones of a freshly killed tiger he had shot.

Fateh was devastated:

> Geoff, it is a massacre [he wrote]. When the police chief showed me the skin, I could not control myself. Tears were rolling down my cheeks. He had to take me away. It's heartbreaking and sometimes I feel guilty that I taught them to have faith in human beings.... All the tigers were shot at point-blank range, just innocently looking at the man with the gun.... Every day some bad news is coming.... Somebody shot a tiger two years ago and somebody else shot one three months before that. It shows that nobody bothered about these animals.

I called Fateh. He was again in tears. "I sometimes think it was my fault," he shouted over the long-distance line. "I taught my tigers not to fear people and see how they have been repaid."

Gopal Moghiya's confession led to the arrests of several others, including his own brother, a Muslim butcher, and four Meena herdsmen who admitted killing four tigers to protect their livestock.

Again, the Forest Department's initial instinct was to cover things up. One or two animals might have been killed, it said, but poaching on such a large scale was impossible. (Gopal Moghiya did eventually recant his confession, yet he had airily bragged of his poaching skills to several disinterested journalists before doing so.)

But the facts could not be denied: eighteen tigers and leopards were already gone from Sariska, perhaps twenty tigers missing at Ranthambhore, and reports of more poaching were filtering in from everywhere. In Uttar Pradesh, for example, where the Forest Department stubbornly insisted that Dudhwa and its adjacent forest still held one hundred and four tigers, Billy estimated there were now no more than twenty.

Valmik did a hasty calculation of the total number of tigers thought to have been poached, based on just five years' worth of official seizures of skins and skeletons. It came to one hundred and twenty animals. And it seems reasonable to assume that several times as many more went unreported.

At that rate, the Indian tiger is surely on its way out. (So, evidently, is the Nepalese: Twenty-five tigers disappeared from the Royal Chitwan Reserve between 1988 and 1990 alone, so large a percentage of the park's resident population that it may be impossible for it ever to recover.)

Tigers have always been poached. Villagers poison them to protect themselves or their livestock, and some skin smuggling has continued despite an international ban on the trade. But compared to the twin menaces of expanding population and dwindling habitat, poaching has been a relatively minor threat to the tiger's survival. Now that has changed. If allowed to continue at its current pace, poaching will swiftly undo whatever good Project Tiger has managed to do over the past two decades.

The immediate crisis was caused by the peculiar demands of Chinese medicine. For hundreds, perhaps thousands of years, tiger bones and other tiger by-products have played an important part in Chinese healing. The catalogue of physical ills which tiger bones and the elixirs brewed from them are supposed to cure includes rheumatism, convulsions, scabies, boils, dysentery, ulcers, typhoid, malaria, even prolapse of the anus. Tiger remedies are also said to alleviate fright, nervousness, and possession by devils. Ground tiger bone scattered on the roof is believed to bar

A vigilant tigress quenches
her thirst at Kanha.

demons and end nightmares for those who sleep beneath it. A "miraculous medicine" made from tiger bone and sold in Vietnam and elsewhere promises "6 love
makings a night to give birth to 4 sons."

The demand for these products is enormous, not only in China and Taiwan, but in
South Korea and in Chinese communities throughout Southeast Asia and some
Western communities as well. A single brewery in Taiwan imports 2,000 kg of tiger
bones a year—perhaps 150 tigers' worth—from which it brews 100,000 bottles of
tiger-bone wine.

The Chinese themselves have finally run out of tigers—a wild population that once
ran into the thousands has been reduced to fewer than one hundred animals—and
so they have begun importing tiger bones on a massive scale, ignoring the complaints of conservationists and willing to pay prices smugglers find irresistible. From
the Indian reserves—where tribal hunters are paid a pittance to take the risks and do
the actual killing—shadowy middlemen, perhaps with the connivance of some Forest
Department and police officials, spirit the bones of poached tigers northward across
the Nepal border, then on into Tibet and China.

More because of the inefficiency of this process, evidently, than out of concern for
the wildlife of other countries, the Chinese have set up a tiger-breeding farm near
Beijing. There, using Siberian tigers obtained from North American zoos, they are
now raising carnivores whose only *raison d'être* is to be disassembled, ground up,
and sold to clients at home and abroad. Its managers predict they'll have bred some
two thousand tigers in the next seven years, and they have recently asked the
Convention on International Trade in Endangered Species for a permit to peddle their
tiger products overseas. "If we don't get the permit," one official told a visitor to the
breeding farm, "we'll just kill all the tigers."

Sentiment aside, some urge that the Chinese breeding program should be encouraged since its success might relieve the pressure on dwindling wild populations.
Opponents argue that farms will never be able to provide enough tigers to satisfy

Chinese demands, while legitimizing trade in tiger products would only make it easier for poachers and smugglers to continue their deadly work.

The Ranthambhore scandal could not have come at a worse time for Project Tiger. Nineteen ninety-three was to be its twentieth anniversary, and a celebration was already planned at which a brand new national census figure was to be announced: 4,300 animals, almost two and a half times the number there had been when the project began.

All the old problems still persisted. The hostility of local people had intensified: arsonists had recently set fires raging through the hearts of Kanha and Nagarahole, where K. M. Chinnappa, the ranger responsible for defending it for so long, had been forced to flee for his life. And there was already one disturbing new problem, a sad side effect of the national struggle with sectional and ethnic separatists that threatens to tear apart the Indian union. Armed militants of one kind or another had taken shelter in seven of the nineteen reserves, intimidating forest staffs, slaughtering animals for fun or food or profit, making a mockery of the parks' supposed inviolability.

Now, massive poaching had been added to that already bleak mix. A three-day International Symposium on the Tiger was to be held in New Delhi in February 1993. Nearly two hundred and fifty delegates were coming from every region of India and many parts of the world, and the government's more strident critics predicted little more than a desperate exercise in defensiveness.

They were wrong. The new All-India Census figure of 4,300 was bravely announced, though almost no one believed it; 3,000 tigers seems a far more realistic figure, according to most of those with whom I spoke, and even that may now be far too high. And the delegates were made to sit through an appallingly self-congratulatory film: "Forest cover is increasing," the narrator intoned. "The tiger reigns supreme"; and in the reserves, "all is well."

Everyone in the hall already knew that all was anything but well, and for the first time in my experience Indian government officials were willing to say so in front of one another and in public. The Forest Secretary, R. Rajamani, set the tone of candor: the anniversary conference, he said, should be an "occasion for introspection, not celebration."

For three full days, the tiger's champions talked and argued and agreed to disagree. Billy had come all the way from Dudhwa, looking out of place as he always does once he leaves his jungle. "I don't know which will outlast the other, the tiger or me," he said with a grin. I told him my money was on him.

Fateh was there, too, newly reinstated in the Forest Department by the courts—"I have my dignity back," he said—but relegated for the moment to a desk job. He kept his trademark Stetson on inside the assembly hall, and, while delivering a paper on the problems of censusing tigers, mimicked in cunning pantomime a forest guard trying to trace a pug mark when he had never before held a pencil. Ullas Karanth, the researcher from Nagarhole, eagerly shook the hands of Billy and Fateh and other Tiger-Wallahs he had only read about, and lobbied hard for a more scientific approach to tiger management. Research should be free and unfettered, he said; India needed objective facts upon which to make its hard decisions.

Valmik Thapar seemed to be everywhere, delivering a battery of papers, demanding complete honesty about poaching and other potential embarrassments, and vowing to defend those forest officials willing to bring them to the public's attention.

Everyone seemed to agree that a much greater effort had to be made to involve local people in the creation and management of parks. The poaching crisis would never have occurred had local people felt they had any stake in the tiger's survival. And both central and state governments seemed serious about undertaking ambitious ecodevelopment projects—electricity, water, alternative forms of fuel—to provide benefits at last to the people who live in and around the parks. Some plans seemed so ambitious, in fact, that Ullas Karanth gently pointed out that the government already had access to 96 percent of the country on which to experiment with economic uplift, and might do better to leave alone the mere 4 percent left over for wildlife, while one field director suggested that before government came to the aid of the herdsmen he'd been trying to keep out of his park, he hoped it would at least provide trousers for his forest guards.

There was also a good deal of what seemed to me to be very romantic talk about the importance of maintaining intact the ancient "sustainable lifestyles" of the tribal peoples who live in and around the besieged reserves. I couldn't help but remember the *gujjars* whose herds I'd seen avidly eating up what was left of Rajaji National Park. Their lifestyle was ancient all right, but it was no longer remotely "sustainable"; if Rajaji is to survive, some creative alternative will have to be found for them. If it is not found, the forest will vanish, and so will they. And though every park is unique, it is hard for me to see how the same won't ultimately be true for most if not all of the people now living within India's reserves.

In any case, I left the Delhi conference in better spirits than I had expected. The poaching crisis had brought together the tiger's most eloquent advocates. They were talking to one another now, working together instead of on their own, for the first time more united than divided.

Before flying home to the States, we wanted to revisit Ranthambhore and Dudhwa once again. It had been five years since I had sat on the roof of Valmik's farmhouse watching the village women heading home while he tentatively outlined his plans for the Ranthambhore Foundation. I had been sympathetic then, but privately unconvinced that the hardscrabble landscape around his home could ever be coaxed back to life, let alone that the gulf between wildlife enthusiasts and villagers might one day be breached.

I could not have been more wrong. Valmik's house is now the heart of a green oasis, alive with birds and small animals, shaded by some fifty species of trees, many of them native varieties grown from seeds gathered in the forest. A lush nursery grows 500,000 seedlings for villagers to plant during the monsoon. And a cluster of outbuildings behind the house constitutes a full-scale demonstration farm: a sleek, stall-fed murrah buffalo, already the father of hundreds of handsome progeny scattered through nearby villages; a herd of cross-bred cattle whose milk yield is ten times that of the ordinary Indian cow; heat for cooking provided by a bio-gas plant powered by the animals' dung. Just down the road, village women of all castes and faiths meet in their own handsome, mud-walled building, producing handicrafts which provide needed extra income to some sixty households.

Villagers from as far as fifteen miles away are asking for seeds with which to refor-

Dr. Goverdhan Singh Rathore.

est their land. In at least two villages, the people themselves have formed Forest Protection societies with nurseries of their own. The people of Sherpur, Valmik's nearest neighbors, asked for and then helped dig a cattle ditch two kilometers long so that their approach to Ranthambhore at least can be made as green again as it was in the time of their ancestors.

Valmik is the executive director of the Ranthambhore Foundation and divides his time between his farm and his home in New Delhi, from which he does almost ceaseless lobbying on behalf of wildlife in general and Ranthambhore in particular.

The man in charge of day-to-day activities around Ramthambhore is Dr. Goverdhan Singh Rathore. He is Fateh's son and has his father's chesty swagger and Rajput mustache, but he is a Tiger-Wallah of a different kind: he seeks to serve the tiger by ministering to the needs of those whom he hopes will one day be its protectors.

Five mornings a week he climbs aboard a medical van and sets out for one of fifteen villages. He and his medical team have now offered immunizations and basic health care—heavily dosed with messages about family planning and the importance of preserving the forest—to more than 25,000 people, and more villages have expressed their interest in participating in the program.

The Ranthambhore Foundation is just one of many non-governmental agencies now at work around India's parks, but partly because of the park's fame at home and abroad, it has become a symbol for a new kind of Indian conservation effort. The Indian branch of the World Wildlife Fund has launched a similar project of its own just down the road, and as part of a large-scale ecodevelopment plan intended to serve as a model for other parks, the Rajasthan Forest Department has begun planting fodder to be given away to graziers so that they needn't take their animals into the park.

It is the foundation's work with children that seemed to me to hold the brightest promise. When foundation workers began taking jeeploads of them into the park, the children liked the birds and animals well enough, but what first struck most of them was the novel sight of seeing so many intact trees in one place. Born and raised within a kilometer or two of Ranthambhore, in the heart of what had once been a thick forest, many had never seen more than two or three lopped trees at a time, had never realized before just what had been lost to cattle and goats and the woodcutter's ax.

On our last evening at Ranthambhore, Goverdhan took us to the mud-walled children's educational center the foundation has constructed beneath a huge tree on the outskirts of a nearby village. Lit by the white glare of a hissing kerosene lamp, fifteen boys sat in a circle while one of them rattled out a steady rythm on the bottom of an upturned kettle and they all sang a specially written song about the wonder of trees and the importance of caring for the wild animals that lived beneath them.

These boys had come from miles away to spend the weekend and some had ridden two different buses to get there. Represented among them were several of the communities that live around the park—Meenas, *gujjars*, *malis*, Muslims—all eating from the same pot, singing about the same forest.

As we watched and listened from just beyond the circle of light, other voices could suddenly be heard moving along the dark road behind us. Several more boys, hurrying home to their village, had been moved to join in praise of the forest which ultimately only they can save.

Pug marks pattern a Ranthambhore track in the days when it seemed that a tiger might be seen around every curve.

From Ranthambhore, we returned to Delhi, then made the long drive to Dudhwa to visit Billy. The court cases against him seemed at least momentarily forgotten, and late one afternoon, he did something he only rarely does these days: he accompanied us into the park.

Dudhwa seemed especially handsome as dusk approached and as we drove through the red-brown grass—tiger-striped by the smoke from fires deliberately set to char the undergrowth and allow fresh green shoots to spread for the deer to eat—thousands of swallows and bee-eaters tumbled through the air in pursuit of their evening meal.

But the few animals we saw—chital, a herd of thirty swamp deer, a lone sambar calf somehow separated from its mother—seemed frantic with fear, plunging deeper into the forest as soon as they spotted us, evidence perhaps that they had recently been shot at from vehicles that resembled ours. And only once, along all the miles of dusty road we traveled, did we see a set of tiger pug marks.

Gloom seemed almost palpably to settle around Billy's shoulders as we turned off the metaled road that leads out of the park and onto the rutted track to Tiger Haven that runs for two kilometers along the Neora. The sun was hanging very low in the sky now, and as we came around a bend in the river, wisps of mist rose from the elephant grass and its damp sweet smell filled our nostrils.

Billy hissed, "Stop!" and we shuddered to a halt.

A big male tiger lay motionless atop the riverbank, fifty feet across the river, his brassy coat burnished by the dying sun, his opaque eyes fixed upon us.

I stole a look at Billy as he watched the tiger. It seemed almost an invasion of his privacy: Head cocked to one side, smiling, he was rapt, adoring, his face lit up as if he had unexpectedly come upon a lover.

The tiger gazed back at him for a time, then rose slowly to his feet and—stretched out to an almost unbelievable length, belly nearly touching the ground—slipped into the underbrush and disappeared. Under Billy's vigilant eye, this tiger, at least, still occupies his range, still reminds us of what will be lost if the new hopes stirred at the Delhi conference are allowed to die away.

As the Land Rover started up again, Billy beamed at me and raised one thick thumb in silent delight.

*Pages 168–169:*
Sambar stags (foreground), tails up in alarm, and a herd of surprisingly serene chital watch a male cub pass among them, interested only in cooling himself in the brutal heat of summer by plunging into Rajbagh lake.

# ACKNOWLEDGMENTS

ndian hospitality is limitless, and the list of all the people who have helped Diane and me one way or another over the years is far too long to include here. But a few persons must be thanked individually:

Sajni Thukral—Tutu—and her mother, the late Satwant Narang, who provided us with a second home and a second family in New Delhi;

Divyabhanu Sinh Chavda and his wife, Purnima, also in Delhi, whose devotion to Indian wildlife has only been exceeded by their kindness to us;

Fateh Singh Rathore, Valmik Thapar, Goverdhan Singh Rathore, and Avani Patel, as well as Sunny, Ujwala, Gajendra, Nitin, Panditji, Negina, Shamji, and all the other Ranthambhore Foundation field workers;

Billy Arjan Singh, Balram and Mira Singh, as well as Hanif and the rest of the staff at Tiger Haven;

H. S. Panwar and Dr. A. J. T. Johnsingh at the Widlife Institute;

R. L. Singh and Arin K. Ghose, past and present directors of Project Tiger;

and Victor and Tikki Biswas, Ashish Chandola, Amar Commander, K. M. Chinnappa, Chota Chudasama, S. R. Deb Roy, Maneka Gandhi, B. K. Goswami, Peter Jackson, Ullas Karanth, Charles McDougal, B. L. Meena, T. K. and Sankari Menon, Raghu and Meeta Rai, R. Rajamani, Usha Rai, Sunil Roy, Homai Saha, Pallavi Shah, Toby Sinclair, Brijendra and Dawn Singh, John Singh, Ravi Singh, Tejbir Singh, David Smith, Haik Sookias, Mel and Fiona Sunquist, Hashim Tyabji, John Wakefield, Anne and Bob Wright.

I should quickly add that the opinions I express in this book are entirely my own. No one mentioned above necessarily shares any of them with me.

Carl Brandt believed in this book when I wasn't sure I did and I'm grateful to him, as always. I also owe a lot to M. S. Wyeth and Pamela LaBarbiera of HarperCollins, and to the shrewd, sharp eye of Ann Adelman.

Finally, I want to thank my parents, who first took me to India and then made it possible for Diane to see it, too; Shadi Ram Sharma, with whom we look forward to many more Indian journeys; and the Lawtons—Peter, Sheila, Hannah, and India—whose friendship, forged through a shared concern for Ranthambhore's survival, has become one of our most treasured possessions.

Some of the material in this book has appeared over the years in different form in several magazines, and I would also like to thank the editors of those publications, past and present, for allowing me to indulge my fascination with the Indian jungles at their expense—Les Line and Gary Soucie of the *Audubon*; Carey Winfrey of *Cuisine*; Bill Garrett, Bill Graves, Bob Poole, and Erla Zwingle of the *National Geographic*; and Don Mosher and Connie Bond of *Smithsonian*.

*Opposite:* Unaware of the dangers closing in upon him, a male cub surveys the Ranthambhore jungle.

Allen, Hugh. *The Lonely Tiger*. London, 1960.

Ashby, Lillian Luker (with Roger Whately). *My India: Recollections of Fifty Years*. Boston, 1937.

Barras, Colonel Julius. *India and Tiger-Hunting*. 2 vols. London, 1885.

Booth, Martin. *Carpet Sahib: A Life of Jim Corbett*. London, 1986.

Braddon, Edward. *Life in India: A Series of Sketches Showing Something of the Anglo-Indian—the Land He Lives In—And the People Among Whom he Lives*. London, 1872.

Brander, A. A. Dunbar. *Wild Animals in Central India*. London, 1923.

Burke, Norah. *Jungle Child*. New York, 1955.

Burton, Major General E. F. *Reminiscences of Sport in India*. London, 1885.

Burton, Brigadier General Reginald George. *The Book of the Tiger, with a Chapter on the Lion in India*. London, 1933.

Champion, F. W. *The Jungle in Sunlight and Shadow*. London, 1933.

—. *With a Camera in Tiger-Land*. London, 1927.

Corbett, Jim. *Jungle Lore*. London, 1953.

—. *Man-Eaters of Kumaon*. London, 1944.

—. *The Man-Eating Leopard of Rudraprayag*. London, 1948.

—. *The Temple Tiger and More Man-Eaters of Kumaon*. London, 1954.

Courtney, Nicholas. *The Tiger: Symbol of Freedom*. London, 1980.

Eardley Wilmot, Sir S. *The Life of a Tiger*. London, 1911.

—. *Leaves from Indian Forests*. London, 1930.

Fayrer, J. *The Royal Tiger of Bengal. His Life and Death*. London, 1875.

—. *Thirteen Years Among the Wild Beasts of India*. London, 1882.

Fife-Cookson, Lieutenant Colonel. *Tiger-Shooting in the Doon and Ulwar with Life in India*. London, 1877.

Fitzroy, Yvonne. *Courts and Camps in India: Impressions of Viceregal Tours 1921–1924*. London, 1926.

Forsyth, Captain J. *The Highlands of Central India*. London, 1872.

Fraser, Sir Andrew H. L. *Among Indian Rajahs and Ryots*. Philadelphia, 1911.

Gee, E. P. *The Wildlife of India*. London, 1964.

Ghorpade, M. Y. *Sunlight and Shadows*. London, 1983.

Gouldsbury, Charles Elphinstone. *Tigerland: Reminiscences of Forty Years' Sport and Adventure in Bengal*. London, 1913.

—. *Tiger Slayer By Order*. New York, 1915.

Gurung, K. K. *Heart of the Jungle*. London, 1983.

Hastings, Francis Rawdon-Hastings, 1st Marquis of. *The Private Journal of the Marquis of Hastings*. London, 1958.

Hawkins, R. E., ed. *Jim Corbett's India*. New York, 1978.

Hewett, John Prescott. *Jungle Trails in Northern India*. London, 1938.

Hornaday, William T. *Two Years in the Jungle*. New York, 1885.

Inglis, James. *Sport and Work on the Nepaul Frontier, or Twelve Years Sporting Reminiscences of an Indigo Planter*. London, 1878.

—. *Tent Life in Tiger Land. Being Sporting Reminiscences of a Pioneer Planter in an Indian Frontier District*. London, 1888.

Ismail, M. M. *Call of the Tiger*. London, 1964.

Israel, Samuel, and Toby Sinclair, eds. *Indian Wildlife*. Singapore, 1987.

Johnson, Surgeon Daniel. *Indian Field Sports*. London, 1827.

Kipling, J. Lockwood. *Beast and Man in India: A Popular Sketch of Indian Animals in Their Relations with the People*. London, 1891.

Kothari, Ashish (with Pratibha Pande, Shekhar Singh, and Dinlnavaz Variava). *Management of National Parks and Sanctuaries: A Status Report*. New Delhi, 1989.

Lawrence, Sir Walter Roper. *The India We Served*. London, 1928.

Lockwood, Edward. *Natural History, Sport and Travel*. London, 1878.

Lydekker, R. *The Game Animals of India*. London, 1901.

McDougal, Charles. *The Face of the Tiger*. London, 1979.

McNeely, Jeffrey A., and Paul Spencer Wachtel. *Soul of the Tiger: Searching for Nature's Answers in Exotic Southeast Asia*. New York, 1988.

Neff, Nancy A., ed. *The Big Cats*. New York, 1986.

O'Meara, Lieutenant Colonel E. J. *I'd Live It Again*. Philadelphia, 1935.

Perry, Richard. *The World of the Tiger*. New York, 1965.

Pollok, Colonel. *Fifty Years' Reminiscences in India*. London, 1896.

Powell, Arthur Nugent Waldemar. *Call of the Tiger*. London, 1957.

Prater, S. H. *The Book of Indian Animals*. Bombay, 1965.

Project Tiger. *International Symposium on Tiger, India, February 22–24, 1979*. New Delhi, 1979.

Pye-Smith. *In Search of Wild India*. New Delhi, 1993.

Ranjitsinh, M. K. *The Indian Blackbuck*. Dehra Dun, 1989.

Rathore, Fateh Singh, and Valmik Thapar. *With Tigers in the Wild*. New Delhi, 1983.

Rice, William. *Tiger-Shooting in India; Being an Account of Hunting Expeditions on Foot in Rajpootana During the Hot Seasons from 1850 to 1854*. London, 1857.

Ruark, Robert. *Use Enough Gun: On Hunting Game*. New York, 1966.

Russel, Franklin. *The Hunting Animal*. New York, 1983.

Russell, William Howard. *The Prince of Wales' Tour*. London, 1877.

Saharia, V. B. *Wildlife in India*. Dehra Dun, 1982.

Sanderson, G. P. *Thirteen Years Among the Wild Beasts of India*. London, 1882.

Sankhala, Kailash. *Tiger! The Story of the Indian Tiger*. New York, 1977.

Schaller, George B. *The Deer and the Tiger: A Study of Wildlife in India*. Chicago, 1967.

Scott, Jack Denton. *Forests of the Night*. New York, 1959.

Seshadri, B. *India's Wildlife and Wildlife Preserves*. New Delhi, 1986.

Singh, Arjan. *Eelie and the Big Cats*. London, 1987.

—. *The Legend of the Maneater*. New Delhi, 1993.

—. *Prince of Cats*. London, 1982.

—. *Tara: A Tigress*. London, 1981.

—. *Tiger Haven*. London, 1973.

—. *Tiger! Tiger!* London, 1984.

Singh, Colonel Kesri. *One Man and a Thousand Tigers*. New York, 1959.

—. *The Tigers of Rajasthan*. London, 1959.

Smith, A. Mervyn. *Sport and Adventure in the Indian Jungle*. London, 1904.

Stebbing, E. B. *The Diary of a Sportsman Naturalist in India*. London, 1920.

Stebbing, J. *Diary of a Sportsman and Naturalist in India*. London, n.d.

Stewart, Arthur Easedale. *Tiger and Other Game*. London, 1927.

Stockley, Colonel C. H. *Big Game Shooting in the Indian Empire*. London, 1926.

Sunquist, Fiona and Mel. *Tiger Moon*. Chicago, 1988.

Sutton, Richard Lightburn. *Tiger Trails in Southern Asia*. St. Louis, 1926.

Tawahar, Ali Khan. *Man-Eaters of Sundarbans*. London, 1961.

Thapar, Valmik. *Tiger: Portrait of a Predator*. London, 1986.

—. *The Tiger's Destiny*. London, 1992.

—. *Tigers: The Secret Life*. London, 1989.

Tilson, Ronald L., and Ulysses Seal, eds. *Tigers of the World: The Biology, Biopolitics, Management and Conservation of an Endangered Species*. Park Ridge, Minn., 1987.

Toovey, Jacqueline, ed. *Tigers of the Raj: Pages from the Shikar Diaries—1894 to 1949—of Colonel [Richard] Burton, Sportsman and Conservationist*. London, 1987.

Waldrop, General A. E. *Days and Nights with Indian Big Game*, 1923.

Webber, Thomas W. *The Forests of Upper India and Their Inhabitants*. London, 1902.

Weeden, Rev. Edward St. Clair. *A Year with the Gaekwar of Baroda*. Boston, 1911.

Williamson, Captain Thomas. *Oriental Field Sports*. London, 1807.

# CREDITS

Anyone interested in learning more about the activities
of the Ranthambhore Foundation may write to:
The Ranthambhore Foundation, 19 Kautilya Marg,
Chanakyapuri, New Delhi 110 021, India,
or The Ranthambhore Trust, "Grantchester," Linden Gardens,
Leatherhead, Surrey KT22 7HB, United Kingdom.